Studies of the Third Wave

Westview Replica Editions

This book is a Westview Replica Edition. The concept of
Replica Editions is a response to the crisis in academic and
informational publishing. Library budgets for books have been
severely curtailed; economic pressures on the university presses
and the few private publishing companies primarily interested in
scholarly manuscripts have severely limited the capacity of the
industry to properly serve the academic and research communities.
Many manuscripts dealing with important subjects, often representing the highest level of scholarship, are today not econom-
ically viable publishing projects. Or, if they are accepted for
publication, they are often subject to lead times ranging from
one to three years. Scholars are understandably frustrated when
they realize that their first-class research cannot be published
within a reasonable time frame, if at all.

Westview Replica Editions are our practical solution to the
problem. The concept is simple. We accept a manuscript in camera-
ready form and move it immediately into the production process.
The responsibility for textual and copy editing lies with the
author or sponsoring organization. If necessary we will advise
the author on proper preparation of footnotes and bibliography.
We prefer that the manuscript be typed according to our speci-
fications, though it may be acceptable as typed for a dissertation or prepared in some other clearly organized and readable
way. The end result is a book produced by lithography and bound
in hard covers. Initial edition sizes range from 500 to 800
copies, and a number of recent Replicas are already in second
printings. We include among Westview Replica Editions only works
of outstanding scholarly quality or of great informational value,
and we will continue to exercise our usual editorial standards
and quality control.

Studies of the Third Wave:
Recent Migration of Soviet Jews
to the United States

edited by Dan N. Jacobs and Ellen Frankel Paul

During the 1970s the Soviet Union allowed large numbers of
its citizens to emigrate, the first major group allowed to leave
in five decades. The number of emigrés peaked in 1979, with
50,000 persons leaving the USSR--most of them Soviet Jews, most of
them bound for the United States.

This book studies this most recent of three major influxes
of Soviet Jews into the United States. Using case studies based
on six major cities, it considers where the immigrants came from,
why they came, how they feel about the Soviet regime and people,
what their occupations were in the USSR, and how they are adjusting to social and professional life in the United States. Their
responses are compared with those of earlier immigrants to draw
conclusions about the role the "third wave" may play in U.S.
life. The interviews also shed light on current political, social,
and economic conditions in the Soviet Union.

Dan N. Jacobs is professor of political science at Miami
University. Ellen Frankel Paul is assistant professor of political
science at the University of Colorado, currently on leave and associated with The Hoover Institution.

Studies of the Third Wave: Recent Migration of Soviet Jews to the United States

edited by Dan N. Jacobs
and Ellen Frankel Paul

Westview Press / Boulder, Colorado

The editors express their appreciation to Dean C. E. Williamson, College of Arts and Sciences, Miami University, for providing support funds for the preparation of the manuscript and to Jill Rubin for her accomplished typing efforts.

A Westview Replica Edition

Published in 1981 in the United States of America by
    Westview Press, Inc.
    5500 Central Avenue
    Boulder, Colorado 80301
    Frederick A. Praeger, Publisher

Library of Congress Cataloging in Publication Data
Main entry under title:
Studies of the third wave.
    (A Westview Replica Edition)
    1. Jews, Russian, in the United States--Addresses, essays, lectures.
2. Jews in Russia--Politics and government--1917-   --Addresses, essays,
lectures. 3. United States--Emigration and immigration--Addresses, essays,
lectures. 4. Russia--Ethnic relations--Addresses, essays, lectures.
I. Jacobs, Daniel Norman, 1925-   II. Paul, Ellen Frankel.
E184.J5S873   304.8'73'047   80-29250
ISBN 0-86531-143-9

Printed and bound in the United States of America

Proclaim Liberty throughout the land and
to all the inhabitants thereof.

Leviticus 25:10

Contents

Introduction

Dan N. Jacobs

I

The "third wave" of Jewish immigration to the United
States, which began in the 1970s, is completely composed
of emigrés from the Soviet Union. They are distinctive,
inter alia, in that most of them have spent their entire
lives under the tutelage of a communist indoctrination
system that decries the horrors of capitalist America.
Yet, despite their background, they, like their fellows
of the first wave which came to an end in the early
1920s and the second after World War II, have chosen
to embrace the pressure of a new and--what they have
hoped would be--a freer and more propitious life in the
United States.

In the past 100 years, Jews have left Russia for
a variety of reasons: economic, political, family, personal. But an abiding factor in Jewish emigration has
always been the rampant, government-encouraged, often
government-induced anti-Semitism. This has been true
whether the prevailing government has been tsarist or
Soviet.

Jews are scarcely newcomers to Russia. Tradition
has it that some found their way to the Black Sea lit-
toral at the time of the Assyrian and Babylonian defeats.
In the first half of the eighth century, the kingdom of
the Khazari, the dominating political entity in south
Russia, converted to Judaism. However, the greatest
influx of Jews into Russia did not occur until Poland
was dismembered at the end of the eighteenth century
and its eastern part incorporated into Russia.

In addition to all the traditional excuses for anti-
Semitism in Eastern Europe, Russia experienced the so-
called "Judaizing heresy," which challenged the deity
of Christ and gained prominent support in the fifteenth
century in opposition to Orthodoxy. Jews had nothing to

1

_o with the Judaizing heresy; but it made no difference
to Russians who, at all levels of society, were gripped
by the obsession that the anti-Christ and his "Judaizing"
allies stood as a constant threat to Orthodoxy.

In nineteenth century Russia, the Jews were despised
by all elements of the population. Even the "liberals"
hated them: the Slavophiles because they were foreign,
the Narodniki because they were capitalists. Nicholas I
(1825-1855) became the bane of Jewish existence. His
objective was the assimilation of the Jews, which he
attempted to realize by ordering the kidnapping of young
boys and their impressment into military service for
twenty-five years, with the expectation that during that
time they would accept Orthodoxy.

Nicholas was the worst of the nineteenth century
tsars in his treatment of the Jews, but none of them
treated the Jews with an even hand. All aimed for their
elimination as a group. Constantine Pobedonostsev, the
adviser and pedagogue of several of the last tsars, anticipated that the Jews of Russia would be eliminated:
one-third by emigration, one-third by conversion, and
one-third by "death."

By the late nineteenth century, tsarism was in deep
trouble in Russia. Though an alternative had not yet
appeared upon the scene, revolutionary terrorists had
succeeded in blockading Tsar Alexander II in his own
palace, threatening him even there. Attempt after
attempt was made upon his life. He could move at all
only with extreme security precautions. In spite of
these, however, agents of the Narodnaya volya succeeded
in assassinating him. No Jews were directly involved
in the successful attempt, but it was too damaging to
the regime to admit that Russians had dispatched their
own tsar. To blame it on the "foreign" Jews would provide a safer explanation for the terrible act--and offer
a scapegoat on which the population, angered by the harsh
measures, defeats, and inefficiency of the regime, could
vent its anger, thus deflecting that hostility from the
system.

A series of pogroms was ignited. Between 1881 and
1883, well over one million Jews left or were driven
out of Russia--thus beginning the significant Russian-
Jewish communities in the United States and England,
as well as giving a strong positive impetus to Zionism,
many of whose early adherents came from Russia.

After 1883, the immediate threat to the Jews abated;
but in the years that followed, official anti-Semitism

operated more persistently and extensively than ever
before. The civil service, the professions, academia
were all closed to Jews. The infamous numerus clausus,
limiting the number of Jews who could attend sectarian
schools, was invoked. In 1891 all Jews, some 500,000
were ordered out of Moscow. This was the period when
the Protocols of the Elders of Zion, which has since
been used to instill fear and hatred of Jews throughout
the world, was written in Russia. It was the period
when virulent semi-official anti-Semitic organizations,
such as the Black Hundreds, were formed with the avowed
purpose of instigating mass actions against the Jews
as the source of all Russia's troubles. It was the
period of the "blood libel," in which Jews were accused
of using the blood of kidnapped Christian youth in order
to make the Passover matsot. Not only did the government
do nothing to interfere with such vileness, it sponsored
and encouraged it. No wonder hundreds of thousands of
Jews left Russia throughout this period, particularly
after the tsar's followers inspired pogroms against the
Jews in October 1905 in an attempt to deflect the public
from its then heightened revolutionary inclinations.

In spite of the stream of Jews leaving Russia, which
continued until the U-boat attacks in World War I made
sea travel too hazardous; in 1917, at the time of the
Revolution, there were still between five and a half,
and six million Jews in that country.

Russian Jews inside and outside Russia celebrated
the demise of the tsarist regime. But no more than other
Russians could they agree on a successor. Jews were
to be found in leadership positions among all the revolutionary groups. When the Bolsheviks won out and eliminated all other parties, it meant that many politically active Jews joined the hundreds of thousands of others
who left Russia soon after the Revolution.

The policy toward the Jews during the early years
of the Bolshevik regime was contradictory. On the one
hand, the Bolsheviks were opposed to the Jewish, as to
all religions. They closed synagogues and seminaries,
forbade religious instruction, and so forth. On the
other hand, they encouraged Yiddish and Jewish secular-
cultural activities. Yiddish schools, theatres, books,
and magazines, were subsidized by the regime. The content of these came under increasingly close party
scrutiny; but compared with what was to come later, broad
latitude was permitted. And such ambivalence continued
into the late 1920s and 1930s, even when Jews were forced

out of the top echelons of the party and government and
subsequently executed in the Purges. Anti-Semitism was
still regarded as anti-Bolshevism, and the system moved
actively to suppress it, though it is clear that anti-
Semitism remained a constant concomitant of life in
Russia, among Russian workers, peasants, soldiers, and
bureaucrats.

One of the persistent fears harbored by Soviet
leaders is of "unauthorized," i.e., nongovernmental,
contacts between groups in Russia and similar groups
outside Russia. The apprehension is that such relationships will lead to an undermining of the regime's
authority. The Soviets feared that the Jewish desire
for a homeland was bringing them into contact with
foreign Zionists. Accordingly, the leadership decided
in the late 1920s, to present them with a homeland inside the USSR. The place selected, Birobidzhan, was
far from European Russia, where most Jews lived. It
was in a wind-blown, forsaken territory, on the Man-
churian border in an area to which the Russians had only
flimsy claims and which was soon to see battles over
possession between the Russians and the Japanese. Jews
never settled there in great number. Today, it remains
only as a relic of a Soviet attempt to "solve" the
"Jewish" problem by giving the Jews a homeland in Russia,
and a reminder of the long-standing Soviet hostility
to contacts between Jews inside and outside Russia, a
dislike that grew tremendously after the establishment
of the State of Israel in 1948.

The creation of Israel and the overwhelming and
spontaneous reception given its first ambassador to the
USSR, Golda Meyerson, came at a particularly sensitive
time when Stalin was apprehensive about what he saw as
the spread of nationalism in the communist world. Beginning in 1948, Soviet policy toward the Jews, which
had become increasingly restrictive and threatening
during the preceding decade, became oppressive and
inflexible. The number of religious institutions which
had greatly diminished under Soviet rule was even more
sharply curtailed. Yiddish cultural activities were suppressed, and many of the Jewish cultural leaders were
executed. Intense discrimination was instituted against
Jews in all areas of political and professional life.
Anti-Semitism became the unannounced but undoubted policy
of Stalin's regime towards the Jews during his last years.
There is reliable evidence that, just prior to Stalin's
death, he contemplated both a purge of the few Jews

remaining in high places and a general roundup of the
Jewish population, which was to be forcibly and perma-
nently exiled to Birobidzhan.

In the post-Stalin period, as the economy quickened
and Soviet science required skilled economists, mathema-
ticians, and technicians to move it forward, opportunities for Jews to receive a university education and
to achieve professional success increased. However,
such opportunities were largely restricted to those who
had abilities that the regime felt were indispensible.
Even so, it was exceedingly rare that a Jew would ever
be appointed the head of an institute, or even the chair-
man of an academic department. The popular regime-
supported attitude towards Jews was incorporated in the
maxim: Don't hire a Jew. Don't fire a Jew. Don't
promote a Jew.

In the 1960s, those opportunities which had opened
to Jews after Stalin's death began to become more restricted again. In part, this was because more trained
non-Jewish specialists began to graduate from the universities and institutes. As Khrushchev pointedly indicated, "we" no longer need the Jews, because we have
"our own" experts. This process was accelerated after
the Six Day War in 1967, as the Soviet Union increasingly
sought to cement relations with the Arab world.

The Six Day War had one effect on Soviet leadership.
It had quite a different effect on Jews in the USSR. In
many Jews, particularly in those areas that had only
come under Soviet rule in 1939 as a result of the pact
with Hitler, but elsewhere as well among those who still
retained a trace of Jewish heritage, there welled up
a tremendous pride in what Israel had accomplished. A
small handful of Israelis had risen up against vastly
stronger foes and defeated them, expeditiously, and de-
cisively. It was a heady potion, indeed, to Russia's
long quiescent Jews. It gave rise to a determination
among some to join their brethren in Israel, and the
example of few vanquishing many gave them the courage
to make demands upon the Soviet regime. This was, to
those familiar with Soviet totalitarianism, perhaps a
foolhardy undertaking. But many of those who took the
lead were returnees from Soviet slave labor camps. They
had seen the worst that the Soviet Union could do to
them, and they had survived. They did not want to be
returned to Siberia, but it was not an unknown quantity
to them. And if the regime wished to exact the ultimate
punishment, death, that was still preferable to continued

life under the Soviet system.

In the post-World War II period, few people had been allowed to leave the USSR. But now a combination of circumstances developed that caused the authorities to consider letting some of their Jews leave. The Politburo determined to enter into a period of detente with the West, but the protests by Jewish sympathizers in the West projected a rather unseemly image upon which to construct friendly relations with the West. Even more to the point, the USSR sought to import Western technology and other items on a more favorable basis than currently existed. The Soviets were prepared to trade Jews for computers and ultra-modern ball-bearing plants.

Between 1961 and 1970, the total number of Jews that had been permitted to leave Russia was approximately 7,000. But in 1971 alone, 13,022 were allowed to go. In 1972, the figure rose to 31,681, and in 1973, to 34,733. However, in 1974, the United States Congress indicated that it was not prepared to give the USSR the favorable trading terms it sought. Consequently, in 1975, the number of Jews permitted to emigrate fell to 13,222 and to 14,261 the following year. Subsequently, the figures picked up again as the USSR continued to push detente, revived its hopes for more trade, responded to additional internal and external pressures to permit emigration, and possibly decided that getting rid of its Jews was an idea that had merit. In 1979, the number of Jews permitted to leave Russia exceeded 50,000.

However, late in 1979, the Soviet invasion of Afghanistan occurred. The United States reacted with a series of retaliatory measures: a proposed increase in arms expenditures, a reinforcement of nuclear weapons in Western Europe, the restriction upon grain and high technology sales to the USSR, and the boycott of the 1980 Olympic Games.

The Soviet regime responded in a number of ways, including, during the first part of 1980, the curtailing of Jewish emigration. Only about 15,000 Jews reached Vienna through the first six months of the year.

It seemed unlikely, however, that the spigot of emigration would be turned off completely: the USSR still hoped to resurrect detente, it still needed trade with the West and, if it had decided to make Russia judenrein, the urgency to get the Jews out remained.

Certainly the pressures for the elimination of a

Jewish presence in Russia have increased in recent years.
Generally, when some members of a family migrate, the
tendency is for other members to seek to follow, even
though they originally were not highly motivated to depart. But in addition, the Soviet Union has moved in
several directions to push its Jews out. It has reduced by over 50 percent since 1967 the number of Jews
permitted to receive a university education. In 1979,
few, if any Jews, were admitted to Moscow University,
the most prestigious Soviet institution of higher education. Even those few Jews who had been permitted to
head institutes, departments, and journals have seen
their numbers dwindle. Moreover, overt anti-Semitic
propaganda, masked as anti-Zionist, has been published
by the public press and widely disseminated--and in the
USSR nothing comes off the presses that is not party
and government approved.

It has become more and more difficult for Jews to
remain as Jews in the USSR. The alternatives seem, at
this point, to be either to leave or to assimilate. That
tens of thousands are taking the latter course is indicated by the 1979 census. According to the last previous
census in 1970, there were 2,151,000 Jews in Russia. In
1979, the figure was 1,810,000, a decline of 341,000.
It is known that 173,446 Jews left Russia during that
time. What has happened to the other 167,554? Even
assuming a below zero population increase, it seems
likely that tens of thousands of Soviet Jews have simply
stopped being Jews, in addition to the hundreds of thousands who have followed that course during the past six
decades.

II

The studies which follow in Part I of this volume
focus upon the Russian Jews who have helped to fulfill
Pobedonostsev's prophecy by migrating to the United
States in the 1970s, and who settled not in New York,
where over 40 percent of the newcomers have ultimately
landed, but in the smaller American cities of Detroit,
Cincinnati, Baltimore, and Minneapolis-St. Paul. Part II
is comprised of a less systematic, more reflective, and
personal group of papers dealing with the intimate
thought of the emigrés.
The studies in Part I indicate that the newcomers
are different than earlier groups of Russian emigrés in
that they are better educated and less Jewish oriented.

Although most of them have experienced anti-Semitism
and think it increasing inside the USSR, the latter
was not the only, or perhaps even the principal reason
why they left. For most, the principal reason was to
find "better opportunities," both in terms of profession and living conditions. Only to the extent that
anti-Semitism hampered their opportunities was it a
motivation for leaving) but there were other determining
factors as well, primarily political oppression and the
economic shortcomings of the Soviet system. For intellectuals and professionals particularly, the desire for
freedom provided considerable impetus for leaving.

   Earlier groups of Jews also left to find better
opportunities, but they had a much greater sense of their
Jewishness both because of their religious upbringing
and their identity as victims of organized persecution.
To them, America had great significance as a refuge,
as well as a land of opportunity. To a much greater
degree than with the present immigrants, the mere absence of persecution in America compensated for whatever
professional failures and difficulties in adjustment
they experienced. They might not have a job, they might
be standing in bread lines, but was not Russia a worse
nightmare by far? At least they were free to worship
God as they wished. Free!

   Many of the new immigrants did quite well in the
Soviet Union--and while they were held back because they
were Jews, they did not experience pogroms. They had
not done too badly. They were achievement oriented,
and naturally they brought with them high expectations
for almost immediate success in America.

   So they left the USSR to seek better opportunities
and where should they go but to the "land of opportunity," the United States. While most would have gone
to Israel if that was the only alternative, they preferred another course. Israel was an endangered land,
struggling to keep itself alive militarily and economic-
ally. They had had enough of war and shortages. That
Israel was the land of the Jews was attractive, and
clearly some Russians now in America feel guilty that
they didn't go there; but "opportunity" came first.

   Accordingly, having chosen "opportunity," they are
eager for success. Anything that stands in their way--
recalcitrant bureaucrats, their own lack of English,
the need to start at what is considered a lower level
than in Russia--is a source of frustration. They have
given up everything to secure greater opportunity. Now

let's have it. They expect to work hard; very hard,
but they also expect success--and soon. They demand
it. They have suffered long enough.
However, if success is not forthcoming at once,
most do not give up at least not those of less than middle
years. But certain features of American life seem to
grate upon their sensibilities. They complain about
their inability to find a position suitable to their
talents, about the incompetence of job counselors, about
poor language instruction, about American social and
cultural values, education, crime, suburban sprawl, the
shortcomings of public transportation, the unresponsive-
ness of Americans, the general lack of friends, and absence of deep, satisfactory, friendships in the Russian
sense. Yet, few believe that they made a mistake in
coming to the United States. They complained and pushed
in the Soviet Union. Now they are doing the same here.
It is already bringing them considerable success, though
as the studies seem to indicate, more in some places
than in others. In a few years, when they learn American
refinements, they will do even better.
And since Jewish religious and community involvement
is the American way, it is likely that the next, if not
this generation of Russian imigrants will become involved and success oriented in those facets of American-
Jewish life, as well, though many may fall by the wayside
before that occurs.
Although the studies, in general, complement and
reinforce one another, they point out significant differences in reception of the emigrés by the communities
involved. It would appear that host families offer a
valuable mechanism for countering the newcomers' distaste for bureaucrats, as well as providing the friendship and close relations that the Russians miss. Because
"opportunity" is so important, the vocational guidance
personnel need to be particularly sensitive and skilled.
Because language is so essential to satisfy job placement, strong programs are needed.
It would also appear that some communities have
greater success than others in involving the Russians
in community and religious affairs. The evidence is
that progress can be made in this area, in spite of the
lukewarm interest that many of the immigrants seem to
display. In part, this disinterest can be attributed
to the natural feeling of newcomers who are faced with
urgent problems of survival. Overcoming what are seen
as very high and forbidding social and religious barriers,

is perceived as of secondary importance.

The studies have all been undertaken independently with no attempt to coordinate questions, techniques, or objectives. Undoubtedly, in retrospect, the authors would agree that methodological problems often proved perplexing and the hurdles virtually insurmountable. The results are certainly far from definitive; nevertheless, the outcome has been promising. It is hoped these beginnings will prompt a concerted effort to chart the changing attitudes and the adaptation of the new Russians to American life. Our collective experience indicates that if such a study is not begun immediately, this great opportunity will be lost, because the processes of forgetfulness of the past and adaptation to the present have already commenced. While it is true that many Russian Jews are reluctant to participate in such a study, because they fear some hidden, deceptive governmental agency behind the academic cloak; nevertheless, such an effort should be inaugurated, for there is much to learn about human psychology and adaptability from these dropouts from Soviet society.

1

Soviet Immigrants and American Absorption Efforts: A Case Study in Detroit

Zvi Gitelman

Since 1971, over 23,000 Soviet immigrants have come to the United States, the great majority Jews. They constitute the single largest wave of Jewish immigrants since World War II. Coming from a political, economic, and even cultural-social system very different from our own and unknown to most Americans, they present some unique challenges--as well as opportunities--to those in the host society concerned with their absorption and integration. Obviously, never having worked for a private employer, never having paid school tuition or medical fees, and having enjoyed cheap public transportation, subsidized cultural events, and job security, the Soviet immigrants face a shockingly different situation from that which they have always known as normal. Equally shocking is the freedom of expression found in the United States, pleasing to many, but unnerving in its pornographic and deviant expressions, and even in its seeming lack of respect for authority and office.

By now, most of those dealing directly with the Soviet immigrants have come to appreciate the importance of these background factors in shaping the expectations and behavior of the immigrants. However,

Presented at the Annual Meeting of the Conference of Jewish Communal Service, Grossinger, New York, May 30, 1978. I would like to thank Dr. Jerome Gilison of the Baltimore Hebrew College for his comments and Mr. Samuel Lerner of the Jewish Family Service in Detroit for making possible the survey of immigrants.

12

we are still insufficiently aware of how heterogeneous a
group Soviet Jews are, and how this reflects their adjustment in the United States. In fact, Soviet Jewry is
far more heterogeneous than American Jewry. While there
are few differences in dress, language, religious tradition, education, occupational structure or cultural
habits between Los Angeles Jews and Boston Jews, those
of, say, Georgia and Latvia differ in all of these--and
often dramatically so.

   The geo-cultural differences among Soviet Jews are
relevant to immigrant resettlement not only because those
from one region will differ in their values and Jewish
consciousness from immigrants from another area. They
will also differ in their vocational training and experience. We have learned that physicians in a large
Leningrad hospital have been exposed to more sophisticated techniques and equipment than those who worked in
small town polyclinics. Computer technicians in Moscow
are likely to be more advanced than those from Kishinev.
Moreover, different cultures produce different employment and housing patterns. European women work outside
the home to a far greater extent than Central Asian or
Georgian women; European Jews have very small families
and live in apartments, while Asian and Georgian Jews
have larger families and often lived with other units of
the extended family in one-story homes around a courtyard. Thus, geo-cultural variations influence the values
and expectations of immigrants and are therefore
relevant to resettlement.

   There are three broad types of Soviet Jews: 1) those
living in the Western borderlands (and, hence, known as
Zapadniki, or "Westerners") of the USSR: the Baltic
republics, West Ukraine, and Moldavia; 2) those living in
the Slavic "heartland"--the RSFSR (Russia), the Ukraine,
and Belorussia; and 3) Georgian Jews, "Mountain Jews,"
and Central Asian, or Bokharan Jews.

   Having come under Soviet rule relatively recently
from states where Jewish religion and cultural life
flourished right up to the outbreak of World War II, the
Zapadniki are more attached to Jewish identity and
culture than "Heartlanders." Their acculturation and
political socialization have been of shorter duration,
and the percentage of Yiddish speakers among them is much
higher. It is not accidental that the movement for
aliyah in the 1960s started among them, especially in the
Baltic capitals of Riga and Vilnius, and that roughly
one-fourth of the Soviet immigration to Israel comes from

the Baltic republics, though only about 3 percent of the
Jews reside there. This figure is all the more striking
in view of the fact that Baltic Jews make up only 3.6
percent of the immigration to America. This lends cre-
dence to the belief that they are motivated largely by
Jewish considerations to emigrate.

There are significant differences among the various
components of this "western" Jewry. While Baltic Jewry
is basically secular, Yiddish in culture, and with a
strong prewar background of Jewish political activity,
Moldavian Jewry, living in an area formerly part of
Romania, is less urbanized, less educated, more religious and traditional, while Transcarpathian Jewry,
located in what used to be easternmost Czechoslovakia, is
Hungarian culturally, also less urbanized and educated,
and closer to religion. What is common to these groups
is memory of non-Soviet political systems, of vibrant
Jewish cultures, and of active Zionist and other Jewish
political movements and parties. This memory leads more
often to Jewish activity and to emigration than among
other European Jews of the USSR.

By contrast, the "Heartlanders" are the furthest
removed from Jewish tradition and culture. Many are
third and even fourth generation Soviet citizens, and
the last time any sort of Jewish school was available to
them was about forty years ago. Having, for the most
part, lost their Jewish culture, these people are both
consumers and producers of Russian culture, and are the
single most highly educated ethnic group in the USSR,
occupying prominent roles in the Soviet scholarly,
scientific, and cultural--but not political--establish-
ments. Though they constitute 80 percent of the Soviet
Jewish population, they have contributed only about 14
percent of the immigration to Israel (1971-1975), though
their proportion among those leaving the USSR has risen
constantly. They are impelled by political alienation,
economic motivations, and a desire to escape restrictions
on Jews, and so they constitute about 85 percent of those
who immigrate to the United States and Canada, rather
than to Israel.

In sharp contrast to both European groups are the
Asian Jews. Like the Zapadniki, they include at least
three different groups: Georgians, Bukharans, and
"Mountain Jews." The Georgians are only about 3 percent
of Soviet Jewry, but have made up about a quarter of the
immigration to Israel. Georgian Jews are less educated
than those in the European USSR, but are more community

conscious. Their families are tightly knit, extended, and hierarchical; and this has played a large part in "snowballing" the emigration from Georgia. Motivated mainly by traditional Jewish values and visions of Zion, Georgian Jews have emigrated largely to Israel, and roughly half the Jews of Soviet Georgia are to be found in Israel today.[1]

Like the Georgians, Bukharan Jews have a rich Jewish cultural tradition and a long history of Zionist activity and settlement in the Holy land (as do the Mountain Jews). Today there are about 20,000 recent Bukharan immigrants in Israel, largely from the less educated strata. Lacking the community cohesion and militancy of the Georgians, their adjustment to the Israeli economy and society has not been altogether smooth.[2]

Finally, a few thousand Mountain Jews, originating in Dagestan, have recently come to Israel. Largely rural until recent decades, the Mountain Jews have a long tradition of both persecution and militancy. This is a less educated group employed largely as skilled and un-skilled workers, as well as in agriculture. There are very few Central Asian or Mountain Jews in the American immigration, and only a small number of Georgians. They are undoubtedly more comfortable with Israeli culture, and are more easily absorbed by the Israeli economy than they would be in the United States.

We cannot speak with as much certainty about the ideological and political physiognomy of Soviet Jewry, since we lack attitudinal surveys and other measures of social and political opinion. It is sufficient to note that the percentage of Jews among the much-publicized dissident movement is very high--out of all proportion to the number of Jews in even the urban and educated strata. On the other hand, there are almost 300,000 Jewish members of the Communist Party. They constitute 13.7 percent of the Jewish population--among the Russians, only 6.6 percent are party members. While Jews are less than 1 percent of the Soviet population, they are nearly 2 percent of the party membership. As the most urbanized and educated group in the entire country, Jews have a statistically better chance of being party members (nearly a quarter of the party membership has higher education, while only 5.5 percent of the general population does). Secondly, party membership is a prerequisite for holding certain posi-tions--director of a factory or a research institute, etc.--and many people join the party not so much out of

political conviction as to advance their professional
careers. It must be remembered that Jews are very
rarely to be found in the upper and even middle levels
of the professional party apparatus, strengthening the
assumption that much of the Jewish membership is motivated by career considerations, on the one hand, and
recruited because of the professional positions they
hold, on the other. The point is that there is a
pluralism of political attitudes and behavior among
Soviet Jews. Their attitudes toward their position as
Jews in Soviet society, towards Judaism, and towards
Israel are both varied and complex.

It should now be obvious why we may find some
Soviet immigrants viewing others with suspicion or even
distaste and refusing to have much to do with each other.
The Moscow intellectual may feel that he has nothing in
common with the Georgian worker or even the Lithuanian
hairdresser, except the accident of having lived under
Soviet rule, and that such association is demeaning. In
fact, we might expect these differences to be exaggerated
in America. Because the class, educational, and lin-
guistic differences which would have immediately set off
one group from another in the USSR have disappeared, and
all the immigrants are regarded as equally in need of
help, as "refugees," it becomes all the more important
for each immigrant to rescue his former status and keep
it alive, at least within the immigrant group itself.
If the unsophisticated American social worker can't tell
the difference between the Leningrad accent of a
scientist and the Latvian accent of a technician, the
immigrants themselves certainly can. Thus, the immigrants will resist attempts to get them to "cooperate,"
to associate with and help people with whom they feel
they have little in common. If we realize this, we
might adopt subtle, differentiated approaches in dealing
with the immigrants.

Similarly, American professionals, trained in Anglo-
Saxon politeness and styles of interaction, often fail
to realize how parochial is their notion of interpersonal
and bureaucratic relations. Soviet immigrants may demand
and shout, rather than request; but this is normal,
accepted, and even expected behavior for those coming
from a culture where the relationship between official
and citizen, between salesperson and buyer, is automati-
cally assumed to be an adversary one. The official and
the salesperson have power or a desired object, and will
yield it grudgingly and reluctantly. Moreover, in a

highly centralized system, clerks and officials have
painfully little discretionary power; and the first
instinct of the dissatisfied client is to "ask the
boss." The assumption that those with whom they deal
are powerless clerks is transferred to the United States;
so the frequent demands to "see your superior, the
nachal'nik," should not come as a surprise. Perhaps
it may be of some comfort to those working with immigrants that in the 1930s Molotov complained that the
party Politburo, its highest organ, was having to decide
what size nails were to be used in a Siberian factory,
as no one would assume responsibility for the decision
and it was pushed all the way up the line.

EXPECTATIONS AND FULFILLMENT

     Some who have worked with the immigrants feel they
have unrealistically high expectations of a luxurious
life in America. Since the Soviet media portray America
negatively, one might ask whence these expectations
derive? In the absence of empirical research, one can
only speculate that it comes from memories of American
movies shown in the USSR, or as a result of the reflex
of some Soviet citizens which leads them to believe the
opposite of what the Soviet media present. Perhaps these
expectations derive from experiences in Rome, or perhaps
simply from a natural tendency to think of the country
of immigration as a paradise on earth, something immigrants are prone to do, irrespective of country of
origin or of destination. These expectations may be
revised downward after the first few weeks in the United
States; and then more realistic assessment may follow,
punctuated, perhaps, by fits of depression and despair.
     In the summer of 1976, with the aid of the Univer-
sity of Michigan's Center for Russian and East European
Studies and the cooperation of the Jewish Family Service
in Detroit, I conducted a survey among a random sample
of 132 Soviet immigrants in the Detroit area. Among
the issues investigated were immigrants' expectations
of America and the fulfillment of those expectations.
Nearly half the immigrants say their expectations of
America have been fulfilled, and only 9 percent feel
they have not. Thirty-one percent consider them partially fulfilled, and 11 percent are unable to say. Most
immigrants gave political disaffection, anti-Semitism,
family considerations, and desire for economic improvement as their motivations for emigrating. It is among

those who emigrated primarily for family reasons that
the greatest variance is observed in fulfillment of
expectations. They also have the highest proportion
unable to judge whether or not their expectations have
been fulfilled. The politically alienated straddle the
middle categories: the expectations of one-third are
partially fulfilled, of one-half "more or less fulfilled,"
and of 13 percent completely fulfilled.[4]

Except in the case of the twelve people whose expectations were not fulfilled--where at least eight of
them earn less than $400 a month--there is no relation-
ship between income and fulfillment of expectations.
This strengthens the supposition that relatively few
emigrated primarily for economic reasons.

WORK

The immigrants are not altogether pleased with their
present work in the United States.

Satisfaction with Work[5]

	Detroit	East European Immigrants in Israel	Soviets Coming to Israel in	
			1972	1973
Very Satisfied	8.3%	33.8	37	27
Satisfied	19.7	18.8	35	35
Not Very Satisfied	17.4	4.0	18	25
Not at all Satisfied	15.2	Not reported (43.4?)	10	13
Don't Know	39.4	---	--	--

Though in Israel and Detroit the same questions
were asked (in Russian), comparison is difficult because
of the incompleteness of the 1969-1970 Israeli data and
the high percentage of "don't know" responses among the
Detroiters. Apparently, many of the American immigrants
are either unemployed, unsure about their satisfaction,
or unwilling to "complain" to the interviewer.

From the 1972-1973 Israeli data it may be inferred
that satisfaction with work increases with time in the

new country. We also observe that after one year in
Israel (this pertains to the 1973 group) their satisfaction is higher than that of the Detroit group, though,
again, the higher percentage of "don't know" responses
complicates the analysis greatly.

Even with the limitations of the Detroit data, it
is apparent that, as in Israel, it is the better educated
Soviets who have the most trouble finding suitable and
satisfactory employment. They are more dissatisfied
with work than the less educated, and their dissatisfaction arises primarily from the fact that they are not
working in their own fields. Connected with this
some see their wages as too low. The most severe problems are encountered by medical doctors; but, unlike
in some other American cities, engineers and technicians
have managed to find suitable employment.

While only seventeen of the sixty-two women did
not work in the USSR, in America thirty-two women are
not working. Among working males and females, the latter
are somewhat more satisfied, perhaps because their expectations were lower and they could more easily find
work in their less skilled and less specialized fields.

The immigrants remain sanguine about the future.
Almost all of them hope to work in those fields in which
they worked in the USSR, and some aspire to somewhat
higher or different positions. One factory worker
expressed it this way: "I would like to have my own
business. My dream is to sell liquor." A few of the
women who were in low-level white collar positions in
the USSR are content to be housewives in the United
States, indicating that their work in the USSR was perceived as a necessity, not a means of "self-fulfillment."

INCOME

The immigrants are, naturally, concentrated in the
lower income groups. One-quarter report a monthly income of $400 or less, and another 21 percent earn between
$400 and $600. Fully 17.4 percent report no income at
all. These are people being supported by the Jewish
Family Service for six months and more, until they become
self-supporting.

The Zapadniki report significantly higher incomes
than the Heartlanders. While two-thirds of the Heartlanders (and five of seven Asians) earn less than $800
per month, only half the Zapadniki are in this bracket;
while 17 percent of the Heartlanders earn nothing at all,

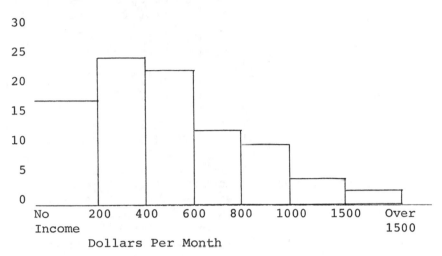

Monthly Income in Detroit

only 8 percent of the <u>Zapadniki</u> are still financially dependent on the JFS. This picture is confirmed by the finding that the <u>Zapadniki</u> possess more consumer goods than the Heartlanders, and the difference between the two groups is greater in the U.S. than it was in the USSR. For example, 83 percent of the <u>Zapadniki</u>, but only 39 percent of the Heartlanders, possess washing machines; a higher proportion of <u>Zapadniki</u> possess every other durable item, including automobiles. There is no significant difference in consumer durable posses- sion between the less and more educated, and since the <u>Zapadniki</u> arrived at roughly the same time as the Heart- landers, their higher incomes and greater possession of durables cannot be explained by the fact that they have had a longer time than Heartlanders "to work them- selves up." Perhaps they benefit from the fact that they have more close relatives in the U.S., and these relatives help them out financially or provide them with some appliances.

As was the case in the USSR, women earn less than men in the USA. Nearly a quarter of the women have no independent income at all, and of the 42 income-earning women, exactly half make less than $400 a month, while of the 59 working men, only 11 (19%) fall into this category. More and less educated immigrants fall pretty

Percentage Possessing[6]

Item	Detroit	E. European After 2 Yrs. in Israel	Israel Immigrants of '74-75 after 1 Yr. in Israel
Refrigerator	74.2*	99.5	--
Tape Recorder	35.6	18.1	16
Phonograph	53.0	21.7	--
Washer	52.0		44
Car/Van	77.3**	27.1	13
TV	81.1	72.5	82

much into the same income categories, largely because the more educated have not yet been able to find work in their specific fields at the professional level that they occupied in the Soviet Union. Nevertheless, some have begun to do so, and this is reflected in the fact that while only 12 percent of the less educated earn more than $800 a month, over a quarter of the better educated are in this income bracket.

It is worth remarking that a higher proportion of those who were dissatisfied in the Soviet Union have consumer durables in the U.S. This may be of some influence on their reported satisfaction/dissatisfaction in the USSR: those who now possess certain items remember the USSR less favorably than those who do not yet possess these items in the United States. The same type of pattern is seen in regard to American income. A somewhat higher percentage of those who say they were basically satisfied with Soviet life have no income or a low income in the United States.

HOUSING

Housing is provided initially by the Jewish Family Service in Detroit. Most immigrants are given apartments in three areas in the suburbs of Detroit, where

---

*Most immigrants live in apartments equipped with a refrigerator and many feel they don't "own" one because it "belongs" to the apartment.

**A car is much more a necessity in the U.S., especially in Detroit.

their rent is subsidized for several months, and furniture is provided. As in Israel, Soviet immigrants are by and large satisfied with the housing.

Satisfaction with Housing[7]

	Detroit	1969-1970 Immigrants in Israel 2 Years After Arrival
Satisfied, Fairly Satisfied, More/Less Satisfied	87.2%	87%
Not so Satisfied Not at all Satisfied	10.6	13
Don't Know	2.3	--

The better educated Detroit immigrants are less satisfied than the less educated: whereas 6 percent of the less educated are not satisfied, 19 percent of the educated are dissatisfied. This may well be due to the better housing the educated enjoyed in the USSR, so that the contrast with American housing is not so sharp. This is borne out by the explicit comparison made. One-quarter of the better educated say their Soviet housing was better than the American and 40 percent said it was about the same, while only 17 percent of the less educated said Soviet housing was superior, and only 24 percent saw it as equal to American housing. It should be borne in mind that the housing provided by the JFS is of uniform quality, so that a levelling occurs among the immigrants, and the better educated may be aware that their status differential has disappeared.

PERCEIVED STANDARD OF LIVING

Half the immigrants perceive their standard of living as having risen in the transition from the USSR to the USA, despite the fact that in many ways they are "starting all over," and "starting from the bottom." Nevertheless, they are acutely aware that though their standard of living may have risen, it is lower than that of most other Americans.

Again, the high percentage of those unable to judge among Detroit respondents makes comparison somewhat difficult, but it is clear that among both groups there is

Change in Standard of Living[8]

	Detroit	1970 Immigrants to Israel from E. Europe After 2 Years
Higher in USA/Israel	49.2	54
Stayed the same	15.2	20
Was lowered in USA/Israel	12.1	27
Don't Know	22.0	--

a rise in standard for most people. However, a significant minority (19%) of the more educated Detroit immigrants feel their standard of living was lowered in the U.S., though 49 percent of both the more and less educated think their standard of living rose. Also, 22 percent of those who were generally satisfied in the USSR say their standard fell in the move to America, while only 5 percent of those dissatisfied in the USSR feel this way, raising the possibility of a projection backwards to the USSR from discontent in the U.S. On the other hand, it is perfectly plausible that those who were satisfied in the USSR felt this way precisely because they had a relatively high standard of living.

While half the immigrants consider their standard of living in the U.S. higher than that in the USSR, an equal proportion perceive their American standard as below the American average. Males, Heartlanders, and better educated immigrants have the strongest perception of having a lower standard of living than the average American.

SOCIAL CLASS

This realistic assessment of their relative position in society is confirmed by their self-assignment to social class in America. Over two-thirds of the immigrants classify themselves as working class or lower class; and while most Americans think of themselves as "middle class," only 19 percent of the immigrants assign themselves to this category. A comparison between self-assigned social class in the USSR and USA illustrates that the immigrants see themselves as having lost considerable social status and having changed their class, with some people unable to define their class in the U.S.

It is striking that a higher proportion of the better educated feel themselves lower class in the U.S., perhaps because of the more radical change in their occupational and--no less important--cultural status.

Self-Ascribed Social Class in USSR and USA

	USSR	USA
Working Class	31.8	45.5
Intelligentsia	42.4	---
Lower Class	0.8	21.2
Middle Class	20.5	18.9
Other	1.5	0.8
Don't Know/No Answer	3.0	12.8

IDENTIFICATION AS JEWS

One of the questions of interest to the Jewish community at large is the degree to which Soviet immigrants identify as Jews once they are resettled. We have very little information on this. In Detroit, we did inquire about the immigrants' synagogue attendance in the USSR and in the U.S. There is considerable change in synagogue attendance habits when the immigrants come to America.

Attendance at Synagogue

	USSR	USA
Often (frequently	8.3	11.4
Sometimes	37.9	43.2
Rarely	---	20.5
Never	52.3	19.7

We should not be misled into thinking that most of the immigrants had suppressed religious tendencies in the USSR and are now able to give them free expression. This is true of a few individuals, but the great majority have gone to synagogue in the U.S. mainly out of curiosity, and because of pressure or invitations by local American Jews. Whereas in the USSR social stigma is attached to synagogue attendance, some American Jews

seem to expect Soviet immigrants to rush to the synagogues, and the immigrants realize this. Moreover, many
American families invite the immigrants to their synagogues and homes for the High Holidays and Passover.
This explains the radical decline in the proportion who
"never" go to synagogue as well as the lesser increase
in more frequent attendance. The Soviet immigrants may
fall into the typical American pattern of synagogue
attendance three or four times a year.

JEWISH FAMILY SERVICE

In contrast to Israel, immigrant absorption in the
U.S. is almost exclusively a nongovernmental function.
The personnel of the agencies dealing with the immigrants
in America are mainly social workers and guidance and
vocational counsellors, rather than civil servants with
no specific vocational training, as is the case in Israel
(where social workers are a small proportion of those
dealing with immigrants). On the other hand, very few
of these American professionals know Russian or have
more than the most superficial acquaintance with the
Soviet background and system from which the immigrants
come.

In Detroit, the Jewish Family Service has overall
charge of the immigrants, and then assigns them to other
services as the need arises. Each immigrant family is
assigned a caseworker. It is likely that over 90 percent
of the Soviet immigrants, even those moving from other
U.S. cities, will have contact with the JFS.

There is no doubt that, for many immigrants, the
relationship with the JFS is not a comfortable one. The
relationship is one of dependence, especially difficult
for those who had a relatively high status in Soviet
life. The immigrants naturally transfer Soviet ways
of dealing with bureaucracies and bureaucrats, and their
confrontationist style quickly alienates--or at least
puzzles--the American social worker. The Jewish agencies
are often perceived as government agencies and the
attitude toward them develops accordingly. There is,
therefore, the possibility that mutual distrust and mis-
understanding will develop between social workers and immigrant. With time, each will learn the ways of the
other; and it is likely that the relationship will become
more comfortable, though the inequality of power and
dependence intrinsic to it--the very word "client" signals
this--militates against a completely relaxed relationship.

In Detroit, respondents were informed by the JFS that we would be asking them for interviews, and though both the JFS and the interviewers took great pains to emphasize that the JFS did not sponsor the interviews, some respondents may have perceived the interviewers as emissaries of the JFS. This would have influenced their response to our inquiry as to their satisfaction with JFS services. Respondents were asked whether they were satisfied or not with the assistance they had received from JFS. Fully 70 percent responded affirmatively, 10 percent negatively, and 17 percent said they were "more or less" satisfied.

The less educated were somewhat more satisfied, probably because their vocational absorption had been easier. Interestingly, satisfaction with the JFS was greatest among those at opposite ends of the income spectrum. Those who have no American income were satisfied, as were those who have a relatively high income; it is the group with the low incomes that is least satisfied. This is because those without income receive JFS financial assistance, while those with higher incomes (over $800 a month) see themselves as having been helped on their way to earning a reasonable wage. Those with the low incomes, on the other hand, no longer receive JFS assistance, but do not earn very much on their own, and would like to continue getting some assistance. They are, therefore, the least satisfied with the Family Service.

ATTITUDES TOWARD AND ASSESSMENTS OF LIFE IN THE UNITED STATES

Respondents were quite ready to detail what troubles them about life in the United States generally, and in Detroit in particular, though almost 20 percent—all of them less educated—could think of "nothing" that disturbed them about life in the U.S. Though Detroit's population is approximately 60 percent black, very few immigrants mentioned any problems they had with this population, perhaps because most of them live in areas where the black population is relatively small. Detroit is sometimes referred to as "the murder capital of the world"—there are more murders per capita in that city than in any other—and quite a few respondents mention crime and fear of walking the streets as serious problems. One respondent suggested that "Detroit needs Soviet order (poriadok) for several months." While a substantial

number of less educated are disturbed mostly by the difficulty of learning English, among the more educated
there are complaints of the low level of culture; and
the latter is connected also with what they consider
to be the provincial character of Detroit: "Detroit
is a village. There is no (public) transportation. A
dead town." Or, as another put it, "I miss the pace
of life in Moscow. Here it's like in the countryside
on vacation."

A frequent complaint is that people in Detroit are
not to be seen on the streets, but only in their cars
and homes. Secondly, they are not as warm, friendly,
and sociable as Soviet people. Interestingly, this
bothers the better educated more than the less educated.
Having thought of America as a land of skyscrapers, they
are surprised at finding "one-story America." A young
man said with some passion that "life here is in home-
fortresses or in individual automobiles. Perhaps this
is peculiar to Detroit, but I can't meet a girl without
an automobile. She's in a car, I'm in a car, what kind
of business is that?" (It should be noted that in this
young fellow's family, which consists of three adults,
there are two automobiles, so we assume he will do
alright with the girls.) People complain about the lack
of public transportation limiting their visits to friends
and relatives. They are disappointed that Americans
do not stroll the streets: "There's no socializing,
transportation. Everything is closed up, you can't go
anywhere on foot. Americans sit at home."

A few observe that they have to work harder in the
United States than in the USSR. One complained about
the lack of biuleteny (sick excuses): "Such a rich
country and it doesn't give the working class a
chance!" Another said: "work, work, work . . . it's not
very interesting."

While mentioning these disquieting aspects of their
new lives, many hasten to add that they are quite pleased
with the political freedom and high standard of living
that they have found.

Asked what they miss from the Soviet Union, more
than half mention friends and relatives, while 15 percent claim they miss nothing at all. Among the better
educated, various aspects of Soviet culture are mentioned; and some return to earlier themes, citing public
transport and social life, or the feelings of safety
in the streets.

Nevertheless, 42 percent of the respondents claim
that there is "nothing" that the United States could
learn from the USSR. Those who do see America bene-
fitting from Soviet examples, and these are mostly
better educated, emphasize discipline and order, and
social services, especially free higher education and
medical services. They recommend instituting the death
penalty, "taking hooligans in hand," and disciplining
youth. ("I never saw naked young girls on the street
in the USSR, and here--just look around, no shame, no
morals, no culture.") One recommended that Americans
"not wash their dirty linen in public. All Soviet
officials have mistresses supported by public funds,
but here everything is published and becomes known to
enemies of the system." (This remark was made when
Congressman Wilbur Mills' escapades were being widely
reported in the press.)

SUMMARY

What emerges from the Detroit study is a picture
of basically satisfied immigrants who are neither blindly
enthusiastic about their new country, nor, for the most
part, blindly negative toward their old one. Despite
the fact that they are at the lower rungs of the economic
ladder, the immigrants are hopeful about their vocational and economic future and feel that they have made
a definite improvement in their standard of living. They
are surprised and disappointed at the provincialism of
Detroit life, at what they see as its low cultural levels.
They are disappointed also in the social styles of
Americans, their tendency to live their social lives
not on the streets, but in the home. They are frightened
and angered--as are the great majority of Americans--
by crime on the streets; and they are dismayed at the
relative lack of public transport, despite the fact that
most of them have their own cars. There is some hesitancy and ambivalence about American individual and
social freedom, and a minority would like to see some
more public order and discipline--as would many Americans.
Both their basic adjustment combined with their criticisms should be heartening to the host society, for they
indicate that this will not be a problematic population;
and, yet, for a while at least, it will retain a healthy
critical perspective which should benefit both immigrants
and host population.

But many important questions are as yet unanswered. We need to know much more about the immigrants' expectations of America, their expectations and evaluations of the resettlement agencies, their socialization--or lack thereof--into the general American community and its Jewish sub-culture. Research into these questions is needed both to make absorption efforts more efficient and effective, as well as to serve the larger interests of the American Jewish and general communities.

NOTES

1. For an anthropological study of a Georgian Jewish community in Israel, see Yitzhak Eilam, Seker Antropologi Shel Hakenhiia Hagruzinit BeAshkelon (Jerusalem: Ministry for Immigrant Absorption, 1974).

2. An anthropological study of the Bokharan immigrants in Israel is Rina Ben-Shaul's Olai Bokhara--Beit Shemesh (Jerusalem: Ministry of Immigrant Absorption, 1975).

3. The data are from "KPSS v tsifrakh," Partiinaia zhizn', No. 10, May, 1976, p. 13.

4. For a detailed examination of the motivations for immigration of the Detroit group, see Zvi Gitelman, "Soviet Jewish Emigrants: Why Are They Choosing America?" Soviet Jewish Affairs, Vol. 7, No. 1 (Fall, 1977). For their views of the Soviet Political system, see Gitelman, "Recent Emigres and the Soviet Political System: A Pilot Study in Detroit," Slavic and Soviet Series (Tel Aviv University), Vol. II, No. 1 (Fall, 1977).

5. Sources: Israel Central Bureau of Statistics, Monthly Bulletin of Statistics--Supplement XXIV, 9 (September, 1973), Table 5, p. 132 and Ministry for Immigrant Absorption, Klitat olai Brih'm betashlag betom hashana harishona lealiyatam (Jerusalem: November, 1974).

6. Sources: Monthly Bulletin, op. cit., Table 9, pp. 136-7; and Klitat Haaliyah, 1975 (Jerusalem, 1976), p. 125.

7. Source: Monthly Bulletin, Ibid., Table 8, p. 135.

8. Source: Klitat Haaliyah, 1972, (Jerusalem, 1973), p. 20.

2 | The Resettlement of Soviet Jewish Emigrés: Results of a Survey in Baltimore

Jerome M. Gilison

The arrival in this country of substantial numbers of immigrants from the Soviet Union has created opportunities for research in several related subjects. Specialists in Soviet society and politics, frustrated for years by the virtual impossibility of doing independent survey research using Soviet respondents, have not been slow to seize the opportunities presented by the influx of former Soviet citizens.[1] From the perspective of the nearly starved Sovietologist, the new wave of immigrants represents a "living data bank" of information about the Soviet system.

For the sociologist interested in the process of cultural adaptation, or "acculturation," however, the new immigrants represent a different kind of "target of opportunity." From this perspective they could be viewed as a case study of individuals in transition between two very different cultures. The relevant variables for this study would be changing attitudes, behavior patterns and developing relationships with native Americans.

The number of Soviet immigrants settling in the United States has substantially increased in recent years. Although present signs indicate a downturn for 1980 compared to the highpoint of 1979, due primarily to worsening Soviet-American relations, there are already sufficient numbers of emigrés in the United States to make large-scale survey research both possible and productive. Indeed, as time passes on, the reliability of information obtained from emigrés about Soviet life is likely to decrease, as it becomes colored by the "Americanization" process, and as salient details are forgotten or confused.

There are several problems associated with obtaining
reliable information about the Soviet Union from the
current wave of emigrés. Having made a conscious decision to reject the country of their birth, they are
likely to relate their experiences in the Soviet society
to certain grievances which formed part of the rationale
for emigration. Furthermore, they have suffered from
the same lack of accessible, accurate information on
their own society that afflicts all Soviet citizens.
They may thus pass on misleading or inaccurate information they received through the media or the widespread
informal rumor network. Their attitudes toward certain
aspects of Soviet life which did not have significant
impact on them personally may also be influenced by such
questionable information.

It should also be remembered that these are Jewish
emigrés--except for the approximately 7 percent who emigrate as the non-Jewish spouse of a mixed marriage. The
special conditions which pertain to the Jewish minority--
and which give its members a qualitatively different
perspective on the Soviet environment--must be taken
into account in assessing the data obtained from this
group. Although they come to Baltimore from many different areas of the Soviet multinational society (fourteen of the fifteen Union Republics), they must be
assumed to have experienced Soviet society, to some
variable extent, through the prism of their Jewish
identity. We must also assume that their perceptions
differ in some respects from those of the majority
nationalities in the areas from which they emigrate.
In this respect, as in others, the Soviet emigrés are
not homogeneous; and the difficulty of interpreting data
obtained from them through survey research can hardly
be overestimated, particularly if one wishes to make
inferences from the data about Soviet conditions in
general.

Difficulties in interpreting data from emigré research result not only from the emigrés' varied experiences of Soviet life, but also from their often
unsettling initial exposure to American life. The
stresses that result from the requirement for rapid adjustment undoubtedly affect their attitudes toward, and
perceptions of, both Soviet and American cultures. Thus
interviews conducted during the initial period of resettlement must be cautiously interpreted, particularly
when the questions probe attitudes toward Soviet and
American societies, and a comparison of the two.

In the summer of 1978 the author conducted a survey
of Soviet emigrés living in the Baltimore metropolitan
area. A random sample of ninety persons was drawn from
the emigré population, with only two restrictions: respondents had to be at least eighteen years old and in
residence in Baltimore for at least four months. As
can be seen from Table 1, migration to Baltimore has
been running at a rate of about 2 percent of the national
total. This is in accordance with the national policy
implemented by the Hebrew Immigration Aid Society (HIAS)
of distributing emigrés in approximate proportion to
the size of the native Jewish population in each city.
At the time of the survey, about 500 emigrés were living
in Baltimore, approximately one-third of the present
emigré population. The sample that was obtained conforms
quite closely to known characteristics of the national
population of emigrés, as determined from data supplied
by national HIAS.

Year	to USA	to Baltimore
1972	453	4
1973	1451	36
1974	3490	88
1975	5250	152
1976	5512	91
1977	6842	175
1978	12265	238
1979	31442	673
TOTAL	66705	1457

TABLE 1. Soviet Jewish Migration,
1972-1979

The primary purpose of the survey was to provide
useful feedback to the agencies involved in resettling
Soviet Jews. Toward this goal, agency workers were
asked at an early stage of the design of the survey
instrument for the kinds of information they would find
most helpful, and their suggestions were incorporated
into the schedule wherever possible. Although the main
focus was thus the resettlement program itself, the survey also revealed much information about the acculturation process during the first few years of the emigrés'
residence in this country. In addition, several questions were included about conditions in the Soviet Union,
mainly as a basis for investigating possible correlations
between the respondents' living conditions in the Soviet

32

Union and relative success in adjusting to the American environment.

Previous work with emigrés and a pilot survey (using a preliminary draft of the survey instrument) revealed that certain direct, evaluative questions were not productive (i.e., the covariance was not sufficient to provide useful information). Thus, a system of indirect questions was developed for those topic areas where there was evidence of difficulty. In some cases an item of data was elicited in two different questions as a method of self-checking. Since the Baltimore survey was originally designed as a pilot for a large-scale multicommunity study, many of the items on the interview schedule were intended for analysis from large sample data. Because this expectation has not been realized, the small sample necessarily limits the statistical inferences that can be reliably drawn from the data obtained. In most cases, the data had to be treated in the aggregate, without division into subsets, because of the small sample.

The data was collected by means of interviews conducted in the respondents' homes by bilingual interviewers who were not previously acquainted with the respondents. A conscious effort was made to set the respondents at ease by creating an atmosphere of informality. The purpose of the survey was explained as an attempt to make improvements in the resettlement program for future immigrants, thus enlisting the respondents' cooperation in the achievement of a positive goal. The survey was also described as a research project done for an academic institution to make it clear that the sponsors were not the very agencies which would be evaluated by the respondents in the interview.

DEMOGRAPHIC PROFILE

Since this survey was designed to sample adult opinion, no one under the age of eighteen was interviewed. The age distribution of the sample was as follows:

Age	Percent of Sample
50 or Over	33
30 - 49	56
18 - 29	11

TABLE 2. Age Distribution of Sample

From this distribution, it would seem that a relatively
high percentage of immigrants are young enough to go
through a period of adjustment and yet look forward to
several decades as wage earners.

A very high proportion of these immigrants comes
from the Ukrainian Republic (Table 3) with the Russian
and Byelorussian Republics following far behind. According to figures from national HIAS, the percentage
of Ukrainians in the national population of Soviet
emigrés is almost exactly the same as in the Baltimore
contingent, i.e., about 70 percent. This fact is of
considerable importance because the Ukraine has been
(and still is) an area of endemic anti-Semitism with
deep roots in the past. In recent years, some of the
most vicious examples of blatant anti-Semitic literature—some of it so offensive that it was eventually
withdrawn--have been published by Ukrainian authors.
As will be seen later, the presence of anti-Semitism
is a major factor in the decision to emigrate.

As can be seen from Table 3, Ukrainian Jews are
twice as likely to emigrate as would be expected from
their proportion of the Soviet Jewish population, while
Russian Jews are under-represented in the emigration
by a factor of three. This disproportion is probably
due to the greater assimilation of Russian Jews than
Ukrainian Jews into the majority culture.

Republic	Percent of Sample	Jewish Population, USSR* (Percent of Total)
Ukraine	70	39
Russia	11	35
Byelorussia	6	7
Moldavia	3	4
Georgia	2	2
Lithuania	2	1
Others	6	12

*from USSR census, 1979

TABLE 3. Distribution of sample and USSR Jewish population by Republic.

The data indicate that this is an urban group, predominantly from cities of 500,000 population, with
relatively large Jewish populations. Surprisingly,
Odessa (Baltimore's official "sister-city" in the USSR)
contributes almost one-third of the total sample. (About

35 percent of the total Soviet migration to the USA comes
from Odessa.) Odessa has had a long history of Jewish
settlement and was a leading Jewish community in tsarist
times.   It was also the scene of a major pogrom in 1905
when approximately 300 Jews were killed and thousands
injured.   In recent times, it has been the Soviet Union's
major port on the Black Sea, and has had more contact
with the outside world (through foreign shipping) than
cities in the interior.   In recent years, over 20 percent
of its entire Jewish population has emigrated, and almost
all have come to the United States.[3]   It should also
be mentioned that Odessa has also been known as a
thriving center for the illegal, "private," secondary
economy where many Soviet citizens earn extra money by
moonlighting.

City of Birth	Percent of Sample
Odessa	29
Kiev	20
Kharkov	4
Moscow	4
Leningrad	4
Other Large City	17
Moderate Size City	12
Towns	9

TABLE 4.   City of birth of emigré sample.

Two-thirds of the group are presently married, and
almost every immigrant arrives as part of some family,
although in some cases the family is incomplete.   Of
those who are or had been married, 13 percent indicated
that it was a mixed marriage (one spouse not Jewish).
Although exact figures are not known, most observers
agree that the rate of intermarriage for Soviet Jews
in the USSR is much higher.   There are 1.5 children per
married couple (but many of the married women are still
of child-bearing age).   The sample consisted of 54 percent males and 46 percent females.

Marital Status	Percent of Sample
Married	67
Divorced or Widowed	17
Single (Never Married)	14

TABLE 5.   Marital status of emigré sample.

As one would expect, Russian is the native language of the large majority, and the Russian language is spoken fluently by 98 percent of the emigrés. Yiddish and Ukrainian are also spoken fluently by a sizable minority. However, those who indicated that Yiddish is their native language are decidedly older than the group average. The fact that Ukrainian is not the native language for anyone in this predominantly "Ukrainian" group is a re-flection of the fact--much regretted by Ukrainian nationalists-- that Russian has replaced Ukrainian as the language spoken in Ukrainian cities.

Native Language		Spoken Fluently
Russian	82%	98%
Ukrainian	0	47
Yiddish	13	30
English	0	28
Others*	5	19

*Georgian, Polish, Lithuanian, etc.

TABLE 6. Languages spoken by emigrés

Only 26 percent had not completed the combined pri-mary and secondary ten year schooling, which is con-sidered the standard in the Soviet Union; and only 8 percent had less than four years of education. Reflect-ing the high priority given to technology in Soviet education, 43 percent of the emigrés had graduated from an institute (technical college) and another 10 percent had graduated from a university. For those who had taken some form of higher education, the most popular subject was engineering, followed by education and economics.

OCCUPATION ANALYSIS: USSR

As shown in Table 7, the emigré group found employ-ment predominantly in skilled occupations related to their schooling. To get a better picture of their actual job responsibilities, the respondents were asked how many workers they supervised.

If the responses can be taken at face value, the data of Table 8 indicate that about one-third of the sample (those supervising more than 10 workers) had achieved positions of high responsibility in the Soviet economy. However, as indicated below, there are good

reasons for believing that these figures are inflated
due to the respondents' desire to look important in the
eyes of the interviewers.

Occupation	Percent of Sample
Engineering*	24
Management	14
Skilled Production	13
Teaching	8
Accounting	7
Health Professions	6

*Engineering in the Soviet Union includes
certain job descriptions that would be
classified as "technician" in the United
States.

TABLE 7. Occupations of emigré sample.

No. of workers Supervised	Percent of Employed Sample
0	41
1-10	24
11-50	25
More than 50	11

TABLE 8. Workers supervised by emigrés.

MOTIVATION FOR LEAVING

For various reasons, the question of why an emigré
chose to leave the Soviet Union and come to the United
States is a sensitive question, and it is the type of
question that might not be answered with candor by every
respondent. Because it was anticipated that direct questions would not necessarily elicit candid answers, a
system of cross-checking between direct and indirect
questions was used. The results are quite revealing.

When asked directly for the most important reason
for leaving the Soviet Union, almost half (48%) said
"discrimination against Jews," only 8 percent said they
wanted a higher standard of living and only 3 percent
said there was a "lack of job opportunities" for them
in the Soviet Union.

Yet a very different picture emerges through indirect inference from other questions. On a series of
fifteen items, the emigrés were asked to rate the quality

of life for themselves, and for other citizens of the
Soviet Union. This question was designed not only to
learn something about conditions in the USSR, but also
to see how the emigrés viewed their own situation in
relation to other Soviet citizens. In other words, if
the respondent viewed his condition as significantly
worse than average, this could be considered an under-
lying grievance and a potential reason for leaving. On
fourteen of the fifteen items, the emigrés rated the
quality of their own lives significantly better or about
the same as the average "Ivan's" life. On only one item
did they rate themselves significantly underprivileged,[4]
and that single item was equality of job opportunities.
This strongly suggests that lack of job opportunities
for themselves was a major source of irritation with
the Soviet system.

USSR Earnings	Percent
Below national average	39
Approx. average range	18
Moderately above average	30
Greatly above average	7
No earnings	6

TABLE 9. Emigrés' monthly average earnings in USSR.

As Table 9 shows, the majority (57%) reported
monthly earnings at or below the Soviet national average,
while only 7 percent reported earnings greatly in excess
of the national average. An additional significant fact
is that 49 percent reported that they had worked in their
last job position in the USSR for at least seven years,
and 20 percent had worked in their last position for
more than ten years.

While this is not unusual for the Soviet economy,
where occupational mobility is comparatively constrained,
the lack of job advancement could be perceived by some
Soviet Jews as further evidence of discriminatory
policies and another persuasive argument for leaving
the country. It is also possible that this group is
above average in personal ambition and thus subjectively
felt more frustrated by the lack of opportunities and
advancement.

This evidence taken together points to a possible
feeling by the emigrés of having been "dead-ended" in
relatively low-paying jobs without much hope of ever
moving further up the career ladder. This situation must

have been particularly frustrating to them, considering
the fact that 53 percent had a complete higher education
and probably expected better treatment in the Soviet
labor market. What explanation does the emigré have for
his occupational disappointment. Primarily he blames
this on the pervasive anti-Jewish atmosphere of his
native land. Thus, the Jewish emigré probably came to
the conclusion that "you can't get ahead in the Soviet
Union (and particularly the Ukraine), if you are a Jew."
   When they tell us that they left the Soviet Union
because of anti-Jewish discrimination, they are certainly
not lying to us. However, they do not mean by this that
they primarily objected to the virtual prohibition
against the practice of Judaism, the closing of synagogues and Jewish schools, and the strong pressure against
the use of Yiddish. The weight of evidence seems to
show that the primary source of disaffection is in the
area of job discrimination, which makes their Jewish
identity an extra burden in competing for the scarce
resources of the Soviet economy, and makes them feel
like second-class citizens. It is reasonable to suppose
that they hope to shed this burden by coming to the
United States. Furthermore, given this motivation for
emigration, it is not difficult to understand why they
chose to come to this country rather than Israel, where
employment opportunities do not seem very promising.

HARRASSMENT IN USSR

   Once a Soviet Jew applies for an exit visa, he
throws his fate into the hands of the Soviet bureaucracy.
The ways of the bureaucracy are mysterious and unpre-
dictable. A particular request may be handled with speed
and efficiency, another may require the intervention
of a visiting U.S. senator, and a third may end up with
criminal proceedings. The rationale for this behavior
by the Sphinx-like Soviet bureaucracy is difficult to
divine, but some probable reasons for harrassment could
include the desire to discourage other Soviet Jews, the
desire to appease Arab opinion and the willingness to
use Jews as a bargaining wedge for concessions from the
West. To this must be added a certain amount of hap-
hazard inefficiency and inertia, and, for good measure,
a dash of willful malevolence.
   The experience of our sample of emigrés also seems
to confirm the puzzling inconsistency of the Soviet OVIR
(visa office) policy. As Table 10 shows, half of the

group was granted exit visas within three months; but
9 percent had to wait more than a year, and few respondents reported a wait of more than two years.

Waiting Period (months)	Percent
1-3	50
4-6	33
7-12	8
More than 12	9

TABLE 10. Time required for issuance of Soviet visa.

Three-quarters of our respondents also suffered
deprivations of various kinds during the waiting period.
Forty-three percent of them lost their jobs after applying for a visa; another 29 percent were subjected to
other forms of official harrassment, and 34 percent reported that some of their friends started to avoid them.
Only 23 percent went through a waiting period that was
free of anxiety-producing deprivations. In one sense,
this retribution makes it easier for the emigrant to
leave by cutting him off from the work and friends that
bind him to the community and by increasing the psychological distance between the emigrant and society. On
the other hand, it sets in motion the defensive reactions
that can be so counterproductive when immigrants arrive
here.

ENGLISH LANGUAGE SKILLS

For several years a full-time English language
school for Soviet Jewish emigrés has been in operation
in Baltimore. On the well-founded assumption that the
acculturation and employability of the emigrés would
be enhanced by rapid acquisition of spoken English, the
immigrants have been required to enroll during the period
they are supported by the Jewish community (up to six
months at first, more recently a maximum of three months).
Although strenuous effort has been made to recruit
incoming Soviet emigrés for the English language classes,
attendance, at the time of the survey, had apparently
not been a high priority for many emigrés, and many had
departed from classes after only a few weeks. Since 71
percent of the sample claimed to have virtually no knowledge of English on the day of their arrival in the

Attendance	Percentage
Never	24
1 Month or Less	17
2 Months	28
3-6 Months	26
More than 6 months	6

TABLE 11. Attendance at English classes.

United States and 93 percent evaluated their own speaking ability on arrival as poor, there would seem to be
an inherent motivation to attend classes from the
beginning.

As we shall see later, those who attended English
language classes found them to be very helpful, and the
rating of the English classes has improved with each
year. Thus, it is apparent that the rather low rate
of attendance at English classes is not due to the immigrants' low opinion of their value, but rather to the
distracting circumstances of their first few months in
Baltimore when many other crucial matters overshadow
the need for regular class attendance. Those who arrive
with a smattering of English in their background may
feel that they can "pick up" English simply by living
here and being exposed to it daily. The evidence (see
Table 12) does show that the longer they live here, the
better their English-speaking ability. "On-the-job"
training in English, television and casual contacts with
native Americans may make up for the lack of formal instruction; but the development of emigré "mini-colonies"
in certain apartment complexes where the Russians are
concentrated probably slows down the process by immers-
ing them in a Russian-speaking sub-culture.

Time in Baltimore	Spoken English score*
Less than 1 year	3.64
1-2 years	4.23
2-3 years	6.36
3-4 years	6.17
4-5 years	7.14

*The mean score for each group as rated by
 interviewers on a scale of 1 to 10, where
 10 = excellent, 5 = fair, and 1 = poor.

TABLE 12. Relation of residence time to English-
            speaking ability.

Obviously, not all occupations require the same level of language ability. One would assume that the professions, highly skilled white-collar positions and retail sales would require a higher proficiency in English than blue-collar production or construction jobs. As Table 13 shows, however, there is a definite positive relationship between English-speaking ability and earning power, even without controlling for relatively nonverbal occupations.

Monthly gross Income ($)	Mean spoken English score
Unemployed	3.40
400 or less	4.41
400-600	5.44
700-900	5.17
1,000-1,200	7.00

TABLE 13.   Language ability vs. earning power.

Thus, the general pattern seems to be that the immigrants who are employable spend several weeks in English classes and then gradually improve their skills by contacts over time with the English-speaking community. As they acquire more English, they also increase their salaries. (But the data do not show that increased English ability is the cause of the increased earnings).

However, there is another group of immigrants which has different problems and different needs, and which has apparently been lost in the shuffle. This group of emigrés (14% of the sample) has the lowest level of language ability and the least formal schooling in the USSR, and they stay away from English classes almost entirely. This group is also elderly, with a mean age of sixty-six and no one under fifty. Probably related to age as well as lack of English, 77 percent of the group is unemployed; and the remainder earn less than $400 per month. Since they are probably not employable (or marginally employable), they have not been able to benefit from on-the-job training in English and, given their difficulty in speaking English, they probably rely on relatives and friends to act as interpreters when necessary. One can only assume that they live within the closed circle of emigré mini-colonies.

The emigrés in this group are also the only ones who overestimate their ability to speak English (i.e., give themselves a higher score than the interviewers give

them), possibly because they do not want to face the
problem. Given their lack of formal education and their
background and age, it seems likely that this group is
fearful of entering a formal, structured learning process
such as English classes, where they might be embarrassed.
The result of little contact with English-speakers and
avoidance of classes is that some of these individuals
were rated as poor in speaking ability after residence
periods of over four years.

OCCUPATIONAL ANALYSIS--USA

If our analysis of the emigrés' motivation for
leaving is correct, getting a better job is first on
the list of expectations that Soviet emigrés bring with
them to the United States. Yet this is the one area
where the immigrant faces the greatest obstacles during
the initial phases of resettlement. For this reason,
the potential for discouragement and disillusionment
is very great. If the typical Soviet emigré is, indeed,
an individual who feels that his talents were insufficiently appreciated in his former home, it is hard to
imagine the despair he must feel when his talents are
shown to have relatively little value on the American
job market.

Due to strenuous efforts by the employment service
of the Jewish community, 58 percent of the emigrés are
placed in their first job within three months of arrival,
and 83 percent are placed within the first six months.
But the level of placement can hardly match the unrealistic expectations of most emigrés. The majority (52%)
report an initial gross income of less than $400 per
month, and 86 percent report that their first income
is less than $600 per month. The average yearly income
(before taxes) for the first placements is $5,700 (or
$475 per month). Given the unfavorable conditions under
which they enter the American labor market, with some
job retraining required, and with poor to fair language
skills, these initial "entry level" placements represent
an enormous effort by the employment service to place
immigrants on a solid footing of self-sufficiency. While
this effort has been largely successful, and while financial independence has been attained for most immigrants
in a remarkably short time, it must be kept in mind that
it is very difficult for an immigrant to express gratitude for help in finding a job which in all respects,
save salary, represents a definite decline from his

former unsatisfactory position in the USSR.

A comparison was also made of first American jobs
and present jobs to see if the emigrés had achieved some
measure of the upward mobility they apparently sought
in coming to America. The data of Table 14 does not
show much upward movement in job skills and status during
the short period of time in which the emigrés have been
employed in this country. On the other hand, there has
been an appreciable increase in the average annual gross
income for the group from $5,700 to $7,782 (excluding
unemployed). This increase in earning power of 37 percent indicates that the immigrants are, on the whole,
proving to be adaptable to the American working environment. Whether they will eventually "move up the ladder"
remains to be seen, but they have not been at work in
America long enough for us to know whether the greatest
success stories will be written by them or by their
children. Even the present modest gains made by the
emigrés should be balanced against two important considerations: (1) with a salary of $7,782 (and many
families with more than one wage-earner), the standard
of living of the average immigrant is measurably improved
over his former Soviet standard; and (2) about two-thirds
of the sample had resided in Baltimore for two years
or less at the time of the survey. This is hardly enough
time for any spectacular improvement in career prospects.

Job Category	Percentage	
	First job	Present job
Unskilled labor	18	14
Skilled production	18	14
Engineering, science	11	11
Retail, service employee	14	14
Professional	4	6
Unemployed	28	34

TABLE 14. Distribution of job skills in emigré group.

In the long run, the possibilities for upward advancement of Soviet emigrés will be limited by age,
language skills, ability to cope with the American work-
place environment and relevant education. A great deal
depends on the drive and ambition of the emigrés themselves, but ultimately it is doubtful that their initial
inflated expectations will be fully realized. Ironically,
living in America will bring these former Soviet citizens
many benefits they never imagined when they applied for

visas, but the one improvement that many of them desired
above all else--the full realization of their working
skills--may never be achieved in America.

ATTITUDES TOWARD SOVIET AND AMERICAN LIFE

Despite the earlier caveats concerning the problems
of interpreting the emigrés' comparative evaluations of
American and Soviet societies, two series of questions
were asked, one directly comparative and the other indirect, concerning relative judgments about the "good-
ness" of aspects of Soviet and American life. Covari-
ation of the two sets is sufficient to indicate that the
judgments are consistent, even when the respondents are
not forced to make a direct comparison. This, of course,
does not give us any assurance that the judgments are
bias-free.

Overall, American society is viewed as superior in
material standard of living, in the quality of the mass
media and in personal freedoms, but is considered inferior in its educational system, cultural life, personal
safety from crime, and climate. There was apparently
some reluctance to score American society lower than
Soviet society in these questions, and quite a few chose
to answer "don't know." This reluctance, however, was
not just due to the presence of an American interviewer.
To acknowledge the superiority of Soviet society in any
respect is, in effect, to call into question the wisdom
of the emigrant's decision to emigrate.

Yet, it was found that emigrés highly valued certain
aspects of Soviet society which they found substantially
superior to American society. It was established by
the data that there was an inverse relationship between
ratings of Soviet society and American society--wherever
one received high marks, the other received low marks.[5]

The negative correlation is so high that one can say
that the emigré found the United States a distinct improvement in all areas where he judged the Soviet Union
to be deficient; but in all areas of life where he had a
high opinion of the Soviet Union, he found the United
States distinctly inferior. Thus it would appear that in
the emigré's mind, the USSR and the USA form polar oppo-
sites in many significant aspects of the quality of life.

Another way of looking at this unanticipated result
is to suggest that the emigré wants to believe that by
coming here, he has removed from his life all the most
disliked aspects of Soviet life. In this way, the

decision to emigrate would be confirmed as a wise decision. Thus, he is probably predisposed to give America
a big plus wherever he found the Soviet Union to be a
minus. On the other hand, there are aspects of Soviet
culture that the average immigrant had accepted while in
the Soviet Union without much thought and which played
little part in his decision to emigrate. Now, confronted
with the sharp contrast of American culture, he finds the
positive facets of Soviet culture brought into sharper
focus and may value them all the more for their absence.
It is, of course, true that a disinterested observer
might make judgments similar to those offered by our
respondents. Having a feeling of greater personal safety
from crime on Moscow's streets than on the streets of
downtown Baltimore need not be explained by reference
to the psychological stresses of adjustment. However,
the consistency with which the two societies are viewed
in starkly contrasting images does suggest that the
polarization of attitudes toward the recently deserted
and the newly adopted societies is in some part serving
psychological needs.

Item	Percent saying USA		
	Better	Worse	Same
Food supply	96	2	2
Housing	96	2	1
Clothing	93	3	3
Newspapers	76	1	4
Jewish-Gentile relations	76	1	4
TV programs	71	4	6
Health care	66	16	8
Friendliness of people	60	11	20
Job opportunities	52	17	11
Sincerity of people	48	9	20
Educational system	37	14	14
Culture	33	20	18
Personal safety from crime	22	34	19
Climate	18	53	27

TABLE 15. Emigrés comparison of USA to USSR.

As can be seen from Table 15, basic material needs
are felt to be much better met in the United States,
and the U.S. media are also found superior by a substantial majority, even though some emigrés are probably
still having problems understanding American entertain-
ment and news standards (and experiencing language

problems as well). One of the most interesting results
in this listing is the relatively high rating given the
United States in "Jewish-Gentile relations" and "job
opportunities." As previously suggested, these are probably the most important reasons for leaving the Soviet
Union and it should be expected that the Soviet immigrant
would be anxious to find evidence confirming the wisdom
of his decision to come to America. Thus he would be
predisposed to see Jewish-Gentile relations in a favorable light, even though he probably doesn't know any
American Gentiles at all. Similarly, 52 percent found
American job opportunities better, even though they had
probably experienced some disappointment in their quest
for employment.

JEWISH IDENTITY AND PRACTICES

From the data, it appears that there are two distinct groups within the emigré community, one of which
has associated itself with the Orthodox Jewish community,
and the other (and larger) of which has not affiliated
at all, although to some extent professing to observe
some Jewish practices in the home. This second group
attends synagogue services rarely, observes some Jewish
holidays, and does not consider itself "religious,"
although it does feel "Jewish."

Synagogue affiliation	Percent
None	69
Orthodox	22
Reform	6
Conservative	2

TABLE 16. Synagogue affiliation of emigrés.

We can thus distinguish between the first group
of "religious Jews" and the second group of "ethnic
Jews." It seems, however, that even the "ethnics" would
like their children to remain Jewish; and some of them
have taken steps in that direction. The emigrés were
also asked some sensitive questions about their children's
relation to religion, even though it was expected that
the presence of an interviewer from a Jewish organization
would tend to bias the answers in a predictable direction.
Thus, although 74 percent said that they wanted a Jewish
education for their children, only 39 percent had actually enrolled their children in a Jewish day school and a
mere 5 percent in Hebrew schools. Half of the parents

said they would disapprove if their child married a
Gentile, while only 17 percent indicated approval.

Type of school children attended	Percent of those with School-age Children
Jewish day school only	39
Public school only	44
Public and Hebrew schools	5
Various, some Jewish	12

TABLE 17.   School attendance of emigré children.

As is generally well known, the emigrés had very
little opportunity to practice or even learn about
Judaism while in the USSR. Only half of our respondents
had ever been in a synagogue in the Soviet Union, and
even though 64 percent acknowledged that they had observed Jewish holidays, it is highly unlikely that they
observed holidays in traditional ways, since both the
means and the knowledge to do so were denied to them.
For example, only 12 percent had learned any Hebrew.
Similarly, even though 58 percent claimed to have learned
about Judaism from parents, the information that was
imparted could not have been very substantial under the
circumstances. It is thus interesting to note that despite their tenuous connection to observable "Jewishness,"
82 percent claim that the majority of their Soviet
friends are Jews. The fact of being a Jew, even when
devoid of any substantial meaning, seems to have played
a large role in their personal relations. While the
anti-Semitism of non-Jews may have been a salient factor
in the surprising "clannishness" of Soviet Jews, it is
hard to escape the conclusion that the feeling of being
Jewish can be crucial in a Soviet Jew's life even without that person knowing anything about Jewish traditions.
It is likely, however, that the Jews who emigrate are
less assimilated than the 90 percent of the Jewish population who have remained (or the 75 percent who have
never asked for Israeli "invitations"). It could be
hypothesized that those Jews who remain in the Soviet
Union have more satisfactory relations with Gentiles,
and thus are less affected by the loss of friends
through emigration. Given the general pattern of intense
friendships in the Soviet culture, the loss of friends
who emigrate could in itself be a significant motivation
for those who are left behind to follow. Emigration in
significant numbers from a particular area could thus be

seen as a stimulus to further emigration. This could
explain, at least in part, the heavy migration from a
few cities like Odessa, which has lost over 20 percent
of its Jewish population through emigration, while
Moscow, with a much larger and more integrated Jewish
population, has lost only about 5 percent.

Even if the majority of these Jews express little
interest in religion as such, they still retain a strong
sense of belonging to the Jewish ethnic group. Eighty-
three percent said that they "feel Jewish but not religious." It is this ethnic sense of Jewishness that they
have brought with them to America.

Finally, it should be mentioned that the emigrés'
whole concept of religion (and, indeed, the word "religion" itself) has been colored by the crude anti-
religious propaganda of the Soviet regime. This propaganda often depicts religious believers as mentally
backward, superstitious fools who believe in "an old,
bearded man in the sky." Anti-religious museums (usually
housed in former churches) have been established throughout the country to demonstrate the absurdity of all
religious beliefs and to present "scientific atheism"
as the rational alternative. Thus, Soviet Jews may very
well come here not only ignorant of Jewish beliefs, but
prejudiced against all religious beliefs.

MEDICAL AND DENTAL CARE

Only 21 percent did not require any medical treatment in Baltimore, and 20 percent visited a doctor more
than ten times. Of those needing medical treatment,
56 percent said that some of the conditions, and 31 percent said all of the conditions requiring treatment
existed before arrival. This indicates that immigrants
arrive here with a backlog of untreated medical problems,
requiring more frequent trips to the doctor than would
normally be expected of a population with this age profile. Of those needing treatment, 85 percent used a
hospital clinic or emergency room, 7 percent were treated
in a doctor's office, and 8 percent were hospital in-
patients.

The same general pattern was found in relation to
dental problems, with only 21 percent not needing any
dental treatment and 23 percent requiring seven or more
visits to a dentist. Both the medical and dental care
received were very high by the immigrants: on the ten-
point scale, medical care received a rating of 8.48

and dental care received 8.14.

It thus appears that the immigrants in our sample have not been well served by the medical and dental services of the Soviet Union. It is probable that the immigrants tended to avoid Soviet medical and dental facilities because of their low opinion of the care they would receive, especially during the emigration period, when they could look forward to better health care abroad. Whatever the cause, the backlog of untreated or incompletely treated medical and dental problems which the emigrés bring with them puts a heavy load on the facilities provided, free of charge, by the American communities.

VIEWS ON RESETTLEMENT PROCESS AND POLICIES

A series of questions was asked concerning opinions about the resettlement process and policies even though such direct questions can lead to "inflated" results. Although the interviewers represented an independent agency (i.e., the Baltimore Hebrew College) with no direct role in resettlement, it is unrealistic to expect that all the respondents made this distinction and gave candid answers. Thus, it should be expected that all views on resettlement work are subject to a certain amount of "inflation," or bias toward favorable evaluations. This is particularly true where general reactions to the American Jewish community were requested. For this reason, the numerical values and percentages that follow should be used for comparative purposes only.

Item	Percentage "Yes"
Felt warmly welcomed	86
Found things different from expectations	51
Found American system confusing	31
Was treated rudely or insincerely	6

TABLE 18. Initial impressions of America.

When asked whether American people or Soviet people are more friendly, 47 percent replied that Americans were more friendly, 23 percent said they are about the same, and only 16 percent said that Soviet people are more friendly. However, in another series of questions Americans were rated significantly higher in friendliness than in sincerity, indicating that some emigrés probably

feel that American friendliness may be somewhat superficial and not genuine.

Problem	Percentage
Learning English	31
Finding a good job	30
Earning enough money	11
Making new friends	5

TABLE 19. Emigrés' biggest problem in resettlement.

     As shown in Table 19, most of the emigrés felt
that the practical problems of learning the language
and finding good employment were the most serious, as
opposed to psychological problems of adjustment or insufficient aid from the American community. (This
response may to some extent reflect the emigrés' reluctance to discuss emotional problems with the interviewer, expressed by shifting the discussion to
relatively mechanical problems.) They also were asked
for their opinions concerning the extent of financial
support presently given to them by the Jewish community.
The vast (and probably exaggerated) majority (84%) said
that the amount of money given them was "just right,"
and only 15 percent felt it was not enough. However,
only a minority (24%) felt that the six-month limit on
assistance is justifiable, with 71 percent supporting
the idea that assistance should be given "as long as
necessary." When asked what (if any) proportion of loans
should be paid back by immigrants, 35 percent said the
entire amount, 52 percent said some part, and 13 percent
said none. Thus, the majority view is that loans should
be considered, at least in part, as gifts.

CHILD-REARING PATTERNS

     If the emigrés are having problems with their chil-
dren resulting from the traumatic uprooting of their
lives, they are not willing to discuss them with our
interviewers: 84 percent of the parents claimed that
they were not having any problems with their children.
Because so few parents were willing to mention any problems at all, no clear pattern emerged. However, it is
known from other sources that some immigrant parents have
indeed experienced difficulties and that some of the
children have been emotionally troubled by the drastic
change in their lives.

The parents in the sample were asked whether they feel there is any difference between Soviet and American methods of bringing up children, and if so, which method is better. Only 6 percent of the parents saw no difference, while 52 percent felt that the Soviet way is better. What these parents had in mind was the greater degree of control which they feel Soviet parents have over their children and the relative permissiveness of the American school and home environment.

For those parents, coming to America has meant a two-fold loss of control over their children. First, they have entered a society in which tight discipline is disparaged and thus very difficult to maintain, and, second, they tend to lag behind their own school-age children in adapting to American culture, particularly in acquisition of fluent spoken English, and thus lose some authority over their children. These problems do not necessarily result in severe conflicts, but they do create some tensions. There is a suggestion in the data (but the sample is too small to permit more certainty) that the longer parents have lived here, the more convinced they become that the Soviet method of child-rearing is superior to the American. If this changing attitude is actually occurring, it may mean that the parents are experiencing more difficulties over time, as their children become "Americanized" in ways that are upsetting to the more "Sovietized" parents.

PRESENT LIFESTYLE OF THE EMIGRÉS

Several questions were asked concerning the present living conditions of the emigrés. The responses are divided in Table 20 to show the changes that take place after the first eighteen months of residence.

	In residence	
Item	Less than 1½ years	More than 1½ Years
Rent an apartment	100%	69%
Own a home	0	28
Have a car, TV, telephone	53	63
Have TV and telephone, no car	28	30
Attend college-level classes	10	0

TABLE 20. Emigrés' present lifestyle.

As the table shows, the acquisition of the standard possessions that typically signify American middle-class

life seems to come at a surprisingly rapid pace to most
immigrants. However, it would be wrong to conclude that
the immigrants have become affluent. Judging from the
locations in which they live, automobile ownership for
most emigrés is virtually a necessity, and in fact 42
percent use their cars to go to work (15 percent use
public transportation and 12 percent walk). While no
attempt was made to learn the value of the cars they
own, one gets the distinct impression that they have
not fared very well in their first ventures on the
American used-car market. Their rapid movement toward
home ownership must similarly be balanced with an apprai-
sal of the kind of home they purchase--and in fact the
good economic sense they show by investing in real property during a time of high inflation. It should also
be kept in mind that these economic gains are usually
won by the pooled efforts of two or more wage earners.
The typical immigrant family consists of a married
couple in their thirties or forties with one or two children, and in 18 percent of the cases, one or more grandparents in the same family unit. In 57 percent of the
cases, the family joined other relatives already living
in the Baltimore area. Only 9 percent of the immigrants
arrive alone, and 12 percent arrive with their children
but without spouse.

Although they acquire the rudiments of middle-class
American life rather quickly, they are still struggling
to climb the ladder, and have certainly not "made it"
in any economic sense. Judging from their average
salaries, they are probably making major purchases on
credit and thus have accumulated financial obligations.
Given the fact that individual income is still insufficient to meet minimal family needs, it is difficult for
most family units to give up the earnings of the wife.
Thus, while this picture is certainly one of solid and
impressive accomplishment, it is far from a picture of
lavish luxury.

FRIENDSHIP PATTERNS

A very large proportion of the emigrés find friends
exclusively within the emigré community during the first
few years of residence in Baltimore. Thirty-six percent
of the entire group have no American friends at all, and
67 percent say that less than 10 percent of their friends
are Americans; 80 percent say that all of their friends
are Jewish. This pattern is quite understandable for the

first eighteen months of resettlement, when language and
adjustment problems absorb all the energies of the immigrants. After the initial period, the situation measurably improves, although the emigrés still remain largely
within their own circles--only half have more than 10
percent of their friendships with Americans. It remains
to be seen whether the emigrés, in the long run, will
develop solid relationships with native-born Americans.
While the concentration of new immigrants in a few apartment complexes has probably prevented loneliness and
isolation during the first few difficult months, the
resulting development of immigrant mini-colonies has
undoubtedly slowed the process of integration into the
American community. However, a relatively slow and
gradual integration process might turn out to be more
beneficial to the immigrants in the long run than
attempts to disperse immigrants and to force them into
more rapid associations with native Americans.

Responses	Time in USA	
	1.5 Years or less	More than 1.5 Years
10% or less American friends*	72%	50%
All Jewish friends	88	63
Closest friends are emigrés	88	63
Had more friends in USSR	83	80
Americans more friendly than Soviets	45	50

*It should be noted that the word "friend" implies
 a closer and more enduring relationship in the
 Russian language than in English

TABLE 21. Friendship pattern of emigrés.

Nevertheless, the picture that emerges from the data
is disquieting. While it is true that the emigrés have
not been in this country long enough to develop many
solid friendships with native Americans--and in many
cases not even long enough to break through the language
barrier--it is still evident that the emigrés are living
in a state of near-isolation from the surrounding society.
There remains the danger that this pattern, once established, may be difficult to alter. Emigré mini-colonies
may be helpful to newly arrived immigrants and may serve
useful purposes during the first one or two years of
residence; but in the longer run, they could become formidable obstacles to successful integration into American
society.

SUMMARY AND CONCLUSIONS

The Soviet emigré is a person in motion between two
cultures. The behavioral lessons he learned in childhood must be learned again as an adult. The stresses
and strains of finding a new life in midstream are very
great, and for some emigrés they are overwhelming. The
survey was not intended to tap that level where psychological stress shows itself. Yet the survey does provide
us with some picture of the acculturation process that
is still taking place. This picture has both its bright
and its dark side.

We find the immigrant rapidly and efficiently given
a start in American society. Within a matter of weeks,
almost all immigrants are living in a new, and, by Soviet
standards, deluxe apartment, with conveniences that are
simply nonexistent in the Soviet Union. Within a matter
of months the employable are employed, the teachable
are being taught, and the elderly are settled and secure.
They rapidly acquire the basic material attributes of
comfortable middle-class life, while continuing to
wrestle with tight family budgets--just like most native
Americans. But this is not the entire picture, only
the surface.

Underneath the surface, the immigrants are far from
being integrated into the American community. Their
friends and acquaintances are mostly other immigrants;
they do not consistently identify either with American
culture or Jewish culture, and they have suffered some
occupational setbacks. It takes about three years for
them to acquire a good command of spoken English, perhaps longer for them to feel comfortable with it. When
the dust clears after the first year of uncertainty and
grappling with the basic problems of survival in America,
the immigrant often finds himself living a life apart
from the natives of his new chosen land. The people with
whom he feels at home--the people who feel at home with
him--are just like him, exiles from the land of their
birth. When they get together, they speak in the
language of that land.

They slowly come to understand that Americans are
both friendly and aloof, cordial and remote, generous and
uninvolved. Particularly in the Baltimore Jewish community, they find that it is difficult for newcomers to
gain entry to the long-standing, almost in-bred relationships that characterize the community.

Yet, despite the formidable problems of adjustment

and the remaining social barriers between themselves and
native American Jews, the emigrés do not seem to have
any grave misgivings about their choice of a new homeland. When asked what advice they would give to someone
still living in the Soviet Union, but just like themselves, 70 percent said they would recommend emigration
to the United States; only 6 percent recommended emigration to Israel, and a scant 1 percent suggested remaining
in the Soviet Union. It appears that a large majority
does not regret the move, despite the problems they have
experienced, and continue to encounter. Certainly, if
they have moments of depression, despair, regret, or
bitterness, they did not reveal those feelings to our
interviewers.

Resettlement agencies and policies of the Baltimore
Jewish community generally found approval from the emigrés; and while their reaction to American society was
mixed, most of their criticisms were directed at aspects
of the American scene which many Americans also find
disturbing. Their biggest complaint about the work of
the resettlement agencies was insufficient individual
care, and this was voiced by only 27 percent of the
sample. Another 11 percent wanted more or better services of various kinds, and 9 percent wanted to fire
some (or all!) of the personnel in the agencies.

Considering the tensions and disappointments of
resettlement, and the potential for misunderstandings
and conflict, the emigrés' basic approval of resettlement
efforts by the resettlement agencies is remarkable. Even
after the earlier caveats about interviewer influence
are taken into account, the approval of resettlement
work is clear and unmistakable.

Thus the resettlement program can be viewed as a
resounding success, if the goal is viewed as a re-
establishment of self-sufficient, functioning family
units, at the lower (but not lowest) rungs of the socio-
economic ladder, living in relative segregation from
native Americans. In the multi-ethnic surroundings of
many large American cities--Baltimore included--this
pattern cannot be considered extraordinary. It may be,
as it was in past waves of Jewish immigration, that the
children will open the doors to American life that the
parents found shut tight.

NOTES

    1. See Zvi Gitelman, "The Third Migration: Profile in Current Research," <u>AAASS Newsletter</u>, Vol. 18, No. 3, Summer 1978, pp. 9-12.

    2. The survey was made possible by a grant from the Associated Jewish Charities and Welfare Fund of Baltimore, the Jewish community organization (Federation), whose agencies (Jewish Family and Children's Service, Associated Placement and Guidance Bureau, and Baltimore HIAS) are primarily responsible for resettlement efforts.

    3. The figures for this and above statements are calculated from data contained in a paper by Eli Valk, "Jewish Emigration from the USSR in 1979" (Soviet Jewry Research Bureau, National Conference on Soviet Jewry).

    4. The correlation coefficient for the two sets of fifteen items was very high (+0.94), indicating that these individuals did not see themselves living a life-style that was markedly different from the average Soviet citizen.

    5. On seven items of societal comparison, the correlation of scores for the two countries was -0.92.

3 | Soviet-Jewish Immigrants in Minneapolis and St. Paul: Attitudes and Reactions to Life in America

Stephen C. Feinstein

The notion of surveying immigrants from the Soviet Union and Eastern Europe is not a new idea. One needs only to refer back to the Harvard University expedition of the post-World War II period to see perhaps the most extensive survey to date which has been carried out by Western analysts.[1] More recently, Professor Zvi Gitelman of the University of Michigan has given new insights into the values and opinions of Soviet immigrants in Israel through the survey he undertook in Tel Aviv.[2] In recent years, however, as the tide of Soviet immigration has shifted from Israel to the United States and Canada, new issues and problems have arisen, particularly among Jewish agencies and communities having direct contact with the newcomers. The initial reaction of many communal circles was to expect another wave of grateful, appreciative "survivors" from Eastern Europe, much like the generation of the post-World War II era, who would immediately begin the process of absorption into American society with the minimal nostalgia for their former homelands. These expectations, however, did not materialize, just as the immigrant's perception of the "efficiencies" of America would suffer severe credibility problems.

Soviet Jewish immigrants began to arrive in the Twin Cities of Minneapolis and St. Paul during 1972. The numbers gradually increased from a handful at first to a community numbering over 200 people in 1977--a

---

General Note: The funding for this survey was provided by a research grant from the University of Wisconsin, River Falls. Special thanks to Peggy Davis, George Bowman, Craig Zabel and Tom Kuetser who carried out the interviews in this project.

substantial number but small compared to the number of immigrants received by larger American cities. Newcomers to the Twin Cities escalated rapidly in the beginning of 1978, jumping to approximately 600 in Minneapolis and 300 in St. Paul by April 1980.

The motivation for the survey undertaken among these new Americans was manifold, but was primarily directed toward documenting the background from which these people came, as well as providing some statistical information on the problems they confronted and the attitudes they developed toward their absorption into American society.

The Minneapolis-St. Paul Jewish community numbers approximately 33,000 people. The predominant base of the Jewish community is composed of descendants of Polish-Russian immigrants who arrived in the early twentieth century, although, like other American Jewish communities, a wave of German-Jewish immigrants was the first into the area during the nineteenth century. Unlike some larger American cities which have received recent Soviet immigrants, the Minneapolis-St. Paul area, with a total population of nearly 2,000,000, is distinctive for its high percentage of white collar and professional jobs and relatively low level of blue collar industry. While job mobility and turnover has always been satisfactory, the recent problems of the American economy have tended to stabilize the Twin Cities' job market more than on previous occasions. Thus, the potential difficulties for outsiders (immigrants or American) coming into the area seeking employment must be viewed as fairly high. This was dramatized among the recent Soviet immigrants as fourteen out of the seventy families which came to the Twin Cities before 1977 moved to different locations within one year of arrival. The relatively low level of industry in the area and the traditional geographic isolation of the Twin Cities has led to less of an influx of ethnic minorities. The predominant population base is German-Scandinavian, with other minorities representing only small percentages of the total population. For example, the Jewish community is less than 2 percent of the total population.

While the Twin Cities offers some potential occupational limitations, the area generally rates as highly desirable because of high living standards and rich cultural atmosphere. St. Paul and Minneapolis possess two nationally known orchestras, over twenty professional and amateur theatre companies, two major art museums, as well as a rich tradition in arts and crafts.

Some immigrants began to appreciate the area more fully
after being part of the community for a year when their
preconceptions of living in "the provinces" or a cultural
wasteland were gradually dispelled. One newcomer remarked that "There was more to do here than in Moscow,
provided you had a car."

If anything appeared appealing at first to most
Soviet immigrants, it was the Minnesota winter. Soviet
Jews generally seem disposed to accept mythology about
what they are capable of tolerating regarding temperature
extremes. Many of the newcomers from the USSR found
the extremely cold winters in Minnesota to their taste
(even before arrival), just as many others have had an
aversion to the "hot" climate of Israel.

With the occupational difficulties plus the general
problems of resettlement not finding easy resolution,
the Soviet Jewish immigrants in the Twin Cities soon
found themselves at odds with the resettlement services
in both cities, and vice versa. It was clear at the
outset that neither side perceived the other as behaving
up to anticipated standards.

It was with these facts in mind that we embarked
at the beginning of 1977, using the title of the University of Wisconsin as entree, to try to establish a
statistical profile of the community. It was quite evident that neither the Jewish Family and Children's
Service* in St. Paul or Minneapolis could embark on such
a project because the antagonisms between the clients
and agency had risen to such heights as to preclude ob-
jectivity. It was also evident that immigrants were
unwilling to speak to representatives of the JFCS lest
frank opinions serve as a potential basis for undermining their dependent relationship. We found, however,
that immigrant families were quite willing to speak to
representatives of a university and indeed they often
spent hours going into meticulous detail about their
life stories and current problems. Only two families
refused to be interviewed, one because the process was
viewed as "useless," and the second because there was
fear of some repercussions on relatives remaining in the
Soviet Union. During early 1977, sixty-six adults (over
age eighteen) were interviewed out of approximately one
hundred and two potential interviewees (64.7%), which
we felt gave a representative sample. Interviews were

*Jewish Family and Children's Service hereafter referred
to as JFCS.

conducted by four students, each of whom had studied
or traveled in the USSR, two of whom were fluent in
Russian and conducted interviews in the native language.

The questionnaire did not seek to repeat the same
or similar questions found in the Harvard project (although some elements of similarity may be observed),
nor did it aspire to seek an encompassing view of Soviet
life. The questionnaire was divided into four sections:
daily life in the Soviet Union, the Jewish experience
in the Soviet Union, the emigration process, and absorption into American society.

As we discovered, some questions which we asked
were superfluous or perhaps naive, while others could
have been phrased better and placed into better form
for collation. However, despite these shortcomings,
it was generally felt by all involved in the project
that sufficient information had been gathered to provide
some of the answers we desired. It must be emphasized,
however, that our interest was more toward the subjec-
tive rather than objective answers, especially in part
four of the questionnaire. When possible, we sought
permission to tape interviews for archival-oral history
purposes. Most newcomers rejected this experience,
although a half dozen found no objection to being
taped for university purposes.

The portrait of the Soviet immigrant which emerged
from the survey in the Twin Cities revealed much expected
information and several noticeable surprises. Forty-
five percent of those interviewed were classified as
"Heartlanders," coming from Moscow or Leningrad, while
24 percent came from the Ukraine, 6 percent from
Byelorussia, with individual cities throughout the USSR
making up the remainder of the group. Striking was the
internal movement which had taken place among the parents
of those interviewed. Eighty-four percent of the fathers
and 76 percent of the mothers of present immigrants were
born in the Pale. More than 60 percent of the fathers
of the present immigrants had held jobs in professional,
medical, or white-collar fields, while 53 percent of
the mothers fell into the same occupational categories.
These figures, especially for women, are quite useful
for suggesting the origin and logic of the work attitudes connected with the current immigrants. While 39
percent of the mothers were occupied as "housewives,"
the high index of professional activity by both parents
would indicate a high level of expectation by the children. This is borne out by occupations in the Soviet

Union: 18.7 percent of those interviewed were occupied
in medical jobs, 48 percent were professionals or engineers, while only 9 percent followed proletarian voca-
tions. When indicating "class affiliation," 89 percent,
an exceptionally high and perhaps suspicious number,
considered themselves as "intelligentsia." A normally
accepted figure for the percentage of "intelligentsia"
in Soviet society is 7 to 8 percent   of the total population.

The high percentage of those who considered themselves intelligentsia was not surprising, as previous
experience with other immigrant studies, both formal
and informal, has suggested that Soviet Jewish immigrants tend to see themselves as "intelligents." When
we asked people to define intelligentsia, the most consistent answer indicated "a person who does mental work
or who works in a creative job." However, the variety
of other definitions suggested that the end definition
was fairly nebulous and could include almost anyone,
perhaps indicating the reason for our high percentage.
For example, according to other definitions we received,
a member of the intelligentsia could be any of the following: "a graduate from a college or technical institute," "anyone with wide cultural interests," "people
who do not believe the government propaganda," "one who
knows about life, not necessarily from a formal education," or "one who always draws his own conclusion."
Of those questioned in our survey, 18 percent thought
that the Soviet intelligentsia embraced between 11 and
20 percent of the total population, while 14 percent
thought the number between 21 and 30 percent. A very
high percentage (32%), however, could not identify the
size of the Soviet intelligentsia. This information is
significant in understanding the immigrant's reaction to
the absorption process in America. Having identified
with the "highest" class in Soviet society, the immigrant
tends to lose class and cultural identity in his new
environment.

The average monthly salary of the sixty-one who
responded to our questions had been 175 rubles a month,
compared to the official 1977 Soviet average of 140
rubles. Clearly, most of the immigrants in the survey
came from a higher standard of living than anticipated.
Twenty-seven percent of those surveyed had owned an automobile in the USSR, compared with the Soviet national
average of 4 percent. Prior to departure from the USSR,
allocation of monthly salary was in proportion to Soviet

national averages: 50 percent of salary was spent on
food, 9 percent on rent, 17 percent on clothing and 8
percent on leisure activities. An exceptionally high
figure of 9 percent savings was indicated by fifty-two
respondents, perhaps indicating the high income level
of our respondents, as well as the general problem of
acquiring consumer goods in the USSR. Reading and
attending theatre, ballet, opera, or movies were listed
with greatest frequency as the major forms of entertain-
ment by the group sample.

   While Soviet immigrants seem to have partaken of
many of the material benefits of life in the USSR, a
high degree of political and religious-national alienation was observable in the responses. Eighty-five percent of those polled felt the Soviet government was
"corrupt." Seventy-nine percent felt it was difficult
for Jews to obtain work in their occupations: 68 percent
indicated existence of discrimination against Jews in
the Soviet educational system which is one of the principal reasons for emigration. Respondents indicated
they thought "it was more difficult to get into a good
school," if one were Jewish, that "Jews must have higher
qualifications than Russians" for entry into special
programs. Physics and subjects relating to international
affairs were generally thought by respondents to be ex-
cluded from Jewish entry. Vocationally, Jewish immigrants indicated that the most difficult areas of Soviet
society to penetrate were: party, diplomatic corps,
military-defense, state security, "higher governmental
positions," nuclear physics, and medicine. Seventy-
three percent of those polled indicated they had felt
social discrimination while living in the USSR. The
frequency of anti-Semitic remarks or insults on social
occasions was noted again and again, while expressions
such as "All Jews should go to Israel" or "Jews should
all be killed" were indicated by several respondents.
Most of those surveyed (71%) felt that the position of
the Jewish community in Soviet society had changed on
several occasions during the past forty years. Several
suggested that things were "not too bad in the thirties"
despite the political purges. Many suggested that the
Jewish position began to worsen noticeably after the
end of World War II and improved only for a short time
after the death of Stalin. In response to an indirect
question, 26 percent of those surveyed felt that from
1967 until the present was the worst period for Soviet
Jews. However, despite the deepening crisis in the

Jewish community in the post-1967 period, only 24 percent
of the respondents indicated they had been involved in
groups concerned with Jewish problems or emigration from
the USSR.   Clearly, the decision to leave was individ-
ualized among families and hence filled with many
anxieties for lack of information about the transitional
process to Western societies.   Forty-six percent of the
respondents were "proud to be a Jew in the Soviet Union,"
and 53 percent "felt at home in the USSR."   This suggests some contradictory reasons as pride in identity
might indicate some willingness to go along with the
society despite its faults.   That more than 50 percent
felt at home in the USSR is a useful figure to gauge
the levels of success and resistance to certain vocational pressures encountered in the United States.

     The typical emigration process for the subjects
in our survey indicated periods of anxiety and waiting,
but not what could be termed tortuous delays.   Ninety-
one percent of those surveyed indicated the decision
to emigrate had been made over "a long period of time,"
and 76 percent indicated that anti-Semitism was the major
reason for beginning the process.   Concern about the
future for children, both educationally and vocationally,
and "freedom" were the items most frequently cited to
amplify this answer.   Forty-four percent of the immigrants received permission to leave the USSR after a
wait of between three and six months, with 24 percent
receiving permission within two months.   Eight respondents (12%) were forced to wait between one and three
years for emigration permits.   The average cost for
visa fees, applications, renunciation of Soviet citizen-
ship, and miscellaneous costs connected with emigration
amounted to 927 rubles per person.   Thirty-two percent
of the respondents indicated it was necessary to receive
financial assistance from friends or from outside the
Soviet Union.   Most immigrants suffered some form of
reprisal for embarking upon the emigration road.   Forty-
six percent of the respondents either lost their job
or quit work because of pressures, 24 percent suffered
harrassment, while others were open to denunciation,
reprimands, loss of friends, and family pressures not
to emigrate (sometimes strong in a mixed marriage).   One
couple was divorced so that a spouse could leave independently of the wife.

     Using the terminology which has emerged to describe
the emigration from the USSR, 91 percent of those in the
Twin Cities community interviewed would qualify as

noshrim (dropouts--those who opted for America over
Israel in Vienna) with the remaining 9 percent yordim
or emigrés from Israel. However, it would seem questionable to label the for·   as dropouts because their
choice of destination had   en more or less determined
before they left the Soviet Union. Sixty percent of
those surveyed indicated the United States was their
first choice. When asked if they would have gone to
Israel if forced to, 71 percent remained willing to do
so, while 27 percent indicated they would not have left
the USSR. This information sheds some important light
on the nature of the recent immigrants. While exposed
to anti-Semitism and many different national pressures
while living in the USSR, Jewish consciousness was not
sufficiently raised by these events to make confirmed
Zionists out of the group. Rather than being dropouts,
it may be said they never intended to go to Israel but
were interested solely in the United States. However,
it must be noted that since the initial survey was completed in mid-1977, the level of Soviet anti-Semitism,
especially in job categories and education, has increased. Informal conversations with post-1977 immigrants seem to indicate that most would have gone anywhere rather than stay in the USSR.

Furthermore, those sensitized tc ewish identity
issues in the USSR appear to have drifted toward Jewish
institutions or identity as a defensive gesture and as
a means of finding out about the emigration movement
itself. Those who had never been to a synagogue in
Moscow or Leningrad before applying to emigrate, often
came to these institutions with enthusiasm after application for a visa. But once they had arrived in America,
as one immigrant put it, "there was no need for the
Jewish community to try to convert us," indicating that
for many identification with Judaism would have to come
gradually. For example, of the forty-five respondents
who experienced anti-Semitism at work, only 24 percent
considered themselves "practicing Jews" in the United
States, though 64 percent had attended synagogues since
their arrival here. Those respondents who indicated
they "did not feel at home in the USSR," indicated a
higher level of practicing Judaism (43%) and synagogue
attendance (83%) since they arrived in America.

Once out of the Soviet Union, the decision to settle
in the Twin Cities appears to have been dependent upon
four factors: 26 percent of the immigrants indicated
family reunification as the reason for settlement; 15

percent came to Minneapolis and St. Paul on the suggestion of friends; 21 percent thought the Twin Cities a
good place to live because of "favorable" climate (extremely cold winters); and 21 percent because HIAS
offered no alternatives.[3] Sixty-seven percent of those
surveyed indicated the Twin Cities had been their first
choice as place of resettlement, while 20 percent indicated they felt there was no choice in the process.

The relationship between the immigrant and the resettlement agencies, in this case, the JFCS in both St.
Paul and Minneapolis, became a matter of concern between
the community and the agencies. An adversary relationship developed between the new arrival and the JFCS
almost from the very beginning, although one can cite
obvious cases where the process was exceptionally smooth.
As a sociological process, the encounters between the
agencies and immigrants are perhaps worthy of a study
of their own, as in no other sphere do the basic
differences between the "new Soviet man" and the American
mentality manifest itself--so much so that on many
occasions the initial meeting between the two sides
might be satirized as showing each party rolling up his
sleeves preparing for the encounter. The result of this
process has been an exceptional amount of stereotyping
by both the immigrants and the agency staffs.

The dualism in the history of the Twin Cities also
provided the dualistic structure of the Jewish agencies
in the area. Drawing funds from community donations,
the two resettlement services offer differing approaches
to the resettlement process. The Minneapolis JFCS, after
experiencing some initial trauma with early Soviet immigrants, developed a program of financial aid provided
on a loan (contractual) basis, with assimilation into
the community being aided by a "host family" program.
The St. Paul agency, on the other hand, maintains a
"grant" policy for a three-month grace period after which
all monies extended are on a loan basis. However, while
technically a loan system, the St. Paul JFCS has never
made any attempts to collect any funds which have been
extended. The theory behind this is the anticipation
that bringing the newcomers into the Jewish community
through charity with a mild sense of obligation will
eventually cause the immigrant to become a contributor
to the community. However, this generally has not
occurred. By 1980, the St. Paul JFCS insisted on manda-
tory contributions from financially well-off immigrant
families who wanted their relatives resettled in the

community. Minneapolis, on the other hand, maintained
a repayment schedule and established a process of billing
newcomers who became independent of the JFCS. The results of this policy were disheartening. Of 142 immigrants billed during 1979 and 1980, only seventy-seven
responded. Fifty-four immigrants were billed three or
more times with no response. Thirty-one, on the other
hand, were making steady efforts to pay off their debt.
Eleven people had paid off their debt completely. The
average outstanding balance by April 1980 was $1172.32
per person, based on 131 people repaying family debt
(outside the federally supported "Block" grant which
was not considered in the loan agreement).

When the initial survey was taken in 1977, the St.
Paul resettlement process did not involve a host family
program, although volunteers from local universities
were used to help integrate the new families into the
community. At the beginning of 1978, partially as a
result of some of the findings in our initial survey,
the St. Paul program moved toward a host family structure. Both agencies sought to bring the immigrant into
American life and employment in the shortest period of
time in order to avoid establishing dependent relationships. Unlike the process in larger American cities
which have received huge numbers of immigrants or like
the case in Israel where standardized language programs
can be developed for groups or newcomers, the erratic
rate of immigration to the Twin Cities before 1979 and
the relatively small numbers, even over a five-year
period, precluded the development of English language
programs specifically geared toward Soviet immigrants.
The result has been that some immigrants are caught in
a pull between work and learning, and the fears which
develop from this are often substantial. A basic question, which haunts agencies and seems to annoy the immigrants, is how the newcomer can learn English and at
the same time diminish the dependent relationship.

The immigrant's reaction to the resettlement process is complex and varied. First, 52 percent of those
surveyed indicated they had been satisfied with the
agency's handling of resettlement, whereas 44 percent
were not. An exceptionally high percentage of immigrants
(74%) felt that the agency personnel did not understand
Soviet immigrants (Only 15% felt they did understand).
Despite this negative feeling toward agency personnel,
62 percent did feel they had been given adequate assistance since their moment of arrival (38 percent no), and

76 percent felt the means of financing the resettlement
was fair. The major difficulty, therefore, seemed to
be a human one, the relationship between the professional
and the Soviet newcomer.

Employment was the area which drew exceptional concern by the immigrants. In 1977, 23 percent of those
surveyed indicated they were unemployed, a high percentage being women who had been employed in the USSR, often
in highly technical jobs. The role of housewife in
America, while sometimes described as a "relief from
the hectic life in the USSR," did become boring especially if the family had had difficulty establishing
friendships with Americans. Only 56 percent of those
surveyed indicated they were happy with the work they
were doing, suggesting a large number were negative or
ambivalent toward their current work. (On this question,
only 9 percent answered "no," while 35 percent rejected
the question.) Breaking down the sample by year of
arrival and reaction to work, it was found, not unpre-
dictably, that job satisfaction was greatest among
those people who had been in the country the longest.
For example, those who arrived in 1973 indicated a 67
percent figure for work satisfaction, the 1974 arrivals
76 percent, the 1975 arrivals 63 percent, while the 1976
arrivals indicated only 32 percent satisfaction.

Immigrants appeared exceptionally critical of the
agencies' emphasis on finding "work," rather than
"employment" or a "profession." Forty-one percent of
the respondents felt they had been forced to compromise
their values on work or lifestyle. Immigrants accused
the agencies of "trying to get rid of immigrants quickly,"
as "treating all Russian immigrants the same," and especially "not understanding the position of the Soviet
doctor." In response to more than half a dozen questions
regarding their problems in America, immigrants continu-
ally emphasized the need for more help in finding
suitable employment. Interestingly, 44 percent of those
surveyed believed that everyone should be guaranteed
a job, while 48 percent did not believe in such guaran-
tees. The current job situation among immigrants also
appears to justify their greatest fear about the process
of becoming new Americans; 42 percent of those asked
"What were your major fears before coming to the United
States?" cited "Unemployment," (Crime and lack of knowledge of the English language followed.); and 35 percent
indicated their fears had been realized. In another
question, which asked "What aspect of American life was

the greatest disappointment to you?" 29 percent indicated "no work or job-related problems" as the most
serious issue. Furthermore, when asked "What aspect
of the Jewish Family Service handling did you dislike
the most?" 36 percent indicated the way they had been
handled in finding employment. Fifteen percent of the
respondents indicated they had turned down job offers,
citing reasons such as poor working conditions, personal
dislike for the job, or that the job was too demeaning.
Of those who were employed, only 49 percent saw themselves making a "satisfactory" salary.

Next to employment, the largest single issue raised
as a problem was the study of the English language. The
introduction to English for the immigrant begins in Rome.
Sixty-eight percent of the respondents indicated they
studied English while in Rome; but only 48 percent felt
it had been helpful, although 36 percent indicated that
the language training received in Rome was the most
significant assistance received in preparation for the
United States. Only 15 percent of the respondents
thought they spoke good English when they came to the
United States.[4] Once in the United States, the average
period of language training was only 2.4 months per
person, usually through a school system course for immigrants from many countries or by private tutor. Sixty-
four percent of those surveyed indicated they could speak
English "adequately" (at the time of the survey), while
58 percent felt "comfortable" speaking English. It
appears that the language difficulties do play an exceptionally important role in preventing an easier transition to American life. Clearly, however, language was
regarded as a secondary problem next to work, although
in many cases intimately linked to success in the work
process. For example, when asked how Jewish Family Service procedures might be improved, 30 percent emphasized
finding employment for newcomers; but no immigrants
mentioned the language issue in answering the question.
Aside from employment, recommendations for improving
the JFCS process emphasized reducing bureaucracy, firing
the present staff, and hiring Russian-speaking personnel.

The social integration of most immigrants in the
Twin Cities indicates a higher level of success than
in language or vocational experiences. Sixty-two percent
of those surveyed thought they had made the right choice
in coming to the Twin Cities, and only 8 percent had
any regrets or reservations about leaving Russia. Seventy
percent of the respondents indicated they were happier

now than when they lived in the Soviet Union, with only
11 percent dissenting. The negative comments about an
immigrant's life in America relate to loss of culture
or position. One respondent commented that "life in
America was too quiet," and another indicated he "was
not happy in Russia and was not happy here either."
Seventy-six percent of those surveyed found they had
a better standard of living in the United States, and
a close 77 percent indicated they ate better in the
United States compared to the Soviet Union.

However, problems in social integration become apparent in an analysis of social contacts between newcomers and Americans. While 91 percent of the immigrants had made friends with Americans, 56 percent felt they
had a better social life in the Soviet Union (Only 23
percent found social life better in America.). Many
immigrants seemd distraught about the lack of sincerity
of Americans and their own isolated lifestyle. To be
sure, Soviet immigrants are somewhat baffled by the fact
that Americans appear insular in their single-family
dwellings, which are characteristic of the Upper Midwest.
Immigrants were annoyed that "Americans said they would
call me up but never did!" On the other hand, newcomers
appeared generally reluctant to initiate a call for a
social occasion except if there was a pressing problem
which they could not resolve themselves. Given the
large number of respondents who identified themselves
as "intelligentsia," it was not surprising to see criticisms of American intellectual attitudes: comments were
frequent about the lack of books in American homes or
apartments (A book is a "true sign" of the intelligentsia
in the USSR.) and the "illiteracy" of Americans toward
"high culture," which could mean anything from antiquity
through twentieth century Russian culture. This reaction
indicates one of the many contradictions associated with
Soviet Jewish immigrants. Their hatred of the Soviet
political system and the anti-Semitism which impelled
them to leave is manifest, yet they do not reject Russian
and Soviet culture. Newcomers are often amazed that
Americans, who have unlimited opportunities to explore,
know little about what they term "elementary subjects."

For those immigrants who were assigned host families
(all in Minneapolis), there seemed to be unanimity that
the presence of a host family was an important factor
in the transition process (88%). The host family's
duties involved meeting the immigrant family upon arrival,
showing them the city, taking them to stores, explaining

various aspects of American purchasing methods (checks, credit cards, credit accounts), assisting in the alloca- tion of expenses, and most importantly, introducing them to other people in the community. In many cases, the host families appear to establish close continuing rela- tionships with the new immigrants.

The existence of the host family tended also to reduce the dependency of the immigrant family on the Jewish Family Service. Host families were often impor- tant in establishing connections which led to job inter- views and in many cases, the job itself. The St. Paul JFS, which did not have a host family program before 1978 appeared to be more subject to the wrath of the immigrants. One immigrant called the personnel "scoun- drels, thieves, bandits, and liars." It would appear that the host family structure serves quite usefully in a pre-emptive fashion by bypassing the agency struc- ture or by lessening the direct blow on the agency personnel by the immigrants. This information, however, does not mean that the host family-immigrant relation- ship was utopian--far from it in many cases. Many host families themselves became frustrated with immigrant pushiness, or insistence upon immediately purchasing a car, several televisions or a house. The most fre- quent object of criticism was the failure to consider a job below one's professional level.

The relationship of the immigrant to American Jews and Jewish institutions was another area where expecta- tions, especially on the part of American Jews, far exceeded the actual level of religious-national identi- fication on the part of the immigrants. The survey of Twin Cities immigrants revealed a very complex portrait of Jewish identity in the USSR, and that complexity was transferred to their community relations in America. While only 18 percent of the group was familiar with Jewish customs or holidays, 52 percent indicated they had attended synagogue; 56 percent spoke or had some understanding of Yiddish, a high figure considering 46 percent of the group sample were from Moscow or Lenin- grad, cities with "assimilated" Jewish communities. In addition, 30 percent of the respondents had some famili- arity with Hebrew, from reading to fluency. These figures indicate a higher than expected familiarity with Jewish life.

Forty-four percent of the immigrants surveyed indi- cated they had developed a stronger identification with Judaism since their arrival; 74 percent admitted to

attending synagogue (No frequency was indicated in the
survey.), and 56 percent now maintained Jewish holidays.
Those who practiced Jewish holidays in the USSR, attended
synagogue, or indicated they did not feel at home in
the USSR, attained the highest percentage of synagogue
attendance in America. On the other hand, of those who
indicated they practiced Judaism in the USSR, only 50
percent maintained they practiced Judaism now, indicating
a net fall off of 50 percent. The major limitation on
this figure is that the definition of "practicing"
Judaism may have a variable meaning from the USSR to
the USA. A greater fall off was noted among those who
attended synagogue in the USSR and who practiced Judaism
now (only 17.6 percent of this group).

While the religion statistics may not lead to any
specific conclusions about the immigrant community other
than to say they have the capacity to become Jews, there
was an interesting relationship between Jewish practices
in the USSR and acceptance of the absorption process.
Ninety-four percent of those immigrants who considered
themselves to have practiced holidays in the USSR were
satisfied with the Jewish Family Services' resettlement,
compared to an overall average of 52 percent satisfaction. Those who indicated experiencing anti-Semitism
at work or in school voiced only 47 to 48 percent satisfaction with the Jewish agencies' activities.

Socially, most immigrants appear to have found
American Jews quite different from themselves. Twenty-
one percent of the newcomers found American Jews
different from non-Jews (no answer--29%), and 85 percent
saw distinctive differences between American and Soviet
Jews. This is an interesting figure as most discussion
until this time centered on how different the Russians
were from American Jews. The Russian immigrants themselves seem to perceive easily this difference. In
addition, some immigrants appeared to be disappointed
in some aspects of Jewish life in America (27%). Some
immigrants were offended by the high cost of synagogue
membership, even though newcomers receive a free membership for one year. American Jews themselves were
criticized by the respondents as "not caring for each
other like Russian Jews" (although another noted that
"Russian Jews don't care for each other like American
Jews"), "being shallow," "not having a strong family
structure" and "for looking down on new immigrants."
Immigrants generally found Americans too individualistic
or self-centered (56%) and more materialistic than Soviet

72

citizens (64%). Undoubtedly, much of the generalization about the lifestyle and manners of American Jews was a result of the general cultural shock of seeing America first hand. Nevertheless, the apparent cynicism evidenced here did not act as any significant deterrent to relative happiness in the USA. Of the sixty respondents who indicated they had experienced anti-Semitism in school, 83 percent indicated they were happier with life in America than in the USSR, despite individual problems they might have had in absorption. A bit of nostalgia or realism, however, seems to have crept into the flow of information back to the Soviet Union. When asked if immigrants advised friends by mail or telephone to leave the USSR, only 21 percent (76%--no) indicated that they did so.

SOME OBSERVATIONS ON THE ABSORPTION PROCESS

The information drawn from the Twin Cities' immigrant community provides a portrait of the newcomers which depicts a difference in standard of living and attitudes from previous immigrant groups to America, and the Upper Midwest in particular. There seems to be no doubt that these people are indeed Jews; but their Jewishness seems a secondary interest, which may become more pronounced in time. Certainly, however, the survey suggests that while these people may have been the object of anti-Semitic persecution, they were not persecuted sufficiently to drive away their cultural and romantic attachment to the Soviet Union. Now most of the newcomers surveyed seemed to have been caught up in a self-centered survival process involved with employment or learning the language up to their own expectation level. As a self-defined "intelligentsia" (real or feigned), there appears to be a certain amount of role playing which the immigrant must carry out in order to re-establish some base in his new community. Often this action appears somewhat theatrical, giving rise to negative reactions by both community and professional workers.

However, despite a certain stubbornness on the part of many immigrants (Twenty percent of the sample indidicated they had been stubborn in dealing with the agencies.), it appears that a hostile relationship is inevitable once the newcomer sees what appears to be an agency person acting not too differently from a Soviet bureaucrat. Carrying over some examples

from his own Soviet experiences, the newcomer expects
the American bureaucrat to be somewhat different. Special educational programs, Russian speaking personnel,
reduction of red tape, an intensive English program, and
a respectable job in line with previous experience are
expected almost immediately by most immigrants, contrary
to frequent statements that they might do any type of
work to be free. When decisions were made which
appeared unfavorable to a particular immigrant's position, the technique of "pounding the fist," quite
familiar to Soviet life, became part of the resettlement
process. On several occasions, at least, bewildered
professionals appeared to have given in to newcomers'
demands, thus beginning a vicious cycle as the news
quickly circulated along the "grapevine" in the immigrant community that officials could be coerced. It
is interesting that in the Twin Cities survey, relations
between client and professional had become so bad on
some occasions that five respondents indicated they
thought the Jewish Family Services were anti-Semitic!

In the end, however, the data acquired from the
Minneapolis-St. Paul immigrant community does suggest
that the majority of newcomers are becoming integrated
into the American system and are achieving a reasonable
and sometimes advanced level of success. (For example,
more than a dozen of those interviewed in the survey
had already purchased homes.) For some, however, being
raised in a totally different environment appears to
have precluded "reprogramming." In some respects, perhaps the best way to generalize about the current
generation of immigrants is to say that most fall into
the category of the "desert generation," in that they
may never reach a point where they will become totally
free of their past.

In the eyes of many American Jews, the more serious
aspect of Soviet-Jewish resettlement, however, appears
to be the question of the "Jewishness" of the immigrants,
or, more particularly, whether and when they will move
voluntarily toward more open participation in community
activities. While immigrants in the Twin Cities' survey
indicated they had had some affinities with Jewish institutions and Jews, they are nevertheless apparently perceived by the native community and by themselves as
being isolated in their new environment. Quite simply,
while economic absorption has worked well generally,
adaptation into the social and religious structure of
the community has not taken place as desired. This has

raised some important questions among American Jews in
the Twin Cities area, especially in Minneapolis, where
projections indicate that the newcomers will number more
than 5 percent of the Jewish community by 1981.

One cannot underestimate the importance of the issue
of "Jewishness," for it has broad implications which
reflect upon the debate of "Israel or the West" for
Soviet Jewish immigrants, levels and structure of financial aid for newcomers, and the more profound question
of criteria for "being Jewish in America." As was the
case in the turn of the century rivalry between the
"established" German Jewish community in America and
the Russian newcomers of that era, the question arises
of whether or not American Jews have any specific rights
to define proper Jewish conduct. Further studies might
investigate the levels of success of absorption into
Jewish life between those newcomers coming to large
cities like New York, Los Angeles, and Chicago, and those
settling in medium-sized cities like Minneapolis-St.
Paul, St. Louis, Cincinnati, and Atlanta. On the surface, one is tempted to suggest that with host families
and a small community environment, the newcomers might
be more easily guided into Jewish life. However, this
may not be the case, as immigrants in larger cities like
New York have established new Russian ghettos where the
pressures and opportunities for assimilation for the
current generation may be less, thus increasing the
possibility of the establishment and maintenance of a
strong nationalistic, if not religious, Jewish outlook.

The current wave of newcomers also appears to be
placing severe strains on Jewish communal and religious
organizations. Family and vocational services, at least
in Minneapolis-St. Paul, are just beginning to comprehend
the outlooks and problems of Soviet Jews, six or seven
years after the first immigrants appeared in the communities. Nevertheless, this difficulty may continue as
such services, especially in smaller communities, cannot
afford to hire professionals with backgrounds in Russian
culture. Synagogues and religious schools also face
new challenges, as part of the burden for stimulating
newcomers to obtain knowledge of Jewish life obviously
falls to them. Since the Twin Cities' survey was completed, synagogues have indicated a sharp fall in membership among newcomers after the free membership period
ended. Soviet Jewish immigrant children do often attend
religious school on a part-time or full-time basis. But
only as long as there is no cost involved. There is no

information available about whether or not Soviet newcomers give charitable donations to the Jewish Federa-
tions or other such organizations. With a touch of
irony, it is significant that the group which has had
the greatest success in the Twin Cities in developing
immigrant interest in Judaism is the Lubovicher movement, which has gone to great lengths in terms of out-
reach, even utilizing "specialists" with knowledge of
Russian language to encourage religious participation
by newcomers.

All of this information suggests the complexity
of the recent wave of immigration of Soviet Jews and
how different this wave of newcomers is compared to previous generations. Certainly, further studies must be
done, not only to evaluate the attitudes and responses
of the newcomers themselves, but to survey the American
Jewish community to evaluate their own perceptions of
themselves and their perceptions about the Soviet
Jewish newcomers. Finally, the recent wave of immigrants flooding to the United States from Viet Nam,
Cambodia, Cuba, and Haiti, and the obvious differences
between those immigrations and the influx of Soviet
refugees, offer a seemingly fruitful area for studies
of outlooks about America and the absorption process.

NOTES

1. Alex Inkeles and Raymond Bauer, The Soviet
Citizen (Cambridge, Harvard University Press, 1959).
2. Zvi Gitelman, "Absorption of Soviet Immigrants," in M. Curtis and Mordecai Chertoff (eds.),
Israel: Social Structure and Change. (New Brunswick.
Transaction Books, 1973), and "Soviet Jews in America,"
in Soviet Jewish Affairs, Vol. 7, No. 1, 1977.
3. Because more than 250 immigrants a year are
being settled in Minneapolis and approximately 75 in
St. Paul, newcomers are accepted now only on the basis
of family reunion.
4. By 1980, however, the impact of Rome had become almost nonexistent, as the time spent by the
emigrant in Italy decreased sharply.

4

The New Soviet Migration in Cincinnati

Ellen Frankel Paul and Dan N. Jacobs

The West has had ample opportunity since the mid-1960s to witness the anguished protests of such dissident Soviet intellectuals as Sinyavsky, Daniel, Sakharov, and Solzhenitsyn. Lamentably, it has been difficult to hear the voices of average Soviet citizens who are neither dissenters with an international reputations, nor individuals of heroic stature willing to jeopardize their existence to awaken the world to transgressions against human rights. The Soviet man remains very much an unknown, largely impervious to the inquisitions of curious Western scholars. Now, with the massive exit of thousands of Russian Jews, which began in earnest in 1969 with a trickle and persisted through 1979 with a veritable flood,[1] we are presented with an intriguing opportunity to probe the political and social attitudes of individuals, the vast majority of whom have lived their entire lives as members of a communist society. Obviously, in studying these emigrés, we are dealing

The authors thank the following for their assistance in preparing this study: Morton Startz, Director, Jewish Family Service of Cincinnati; Ina Glazer, Rochelle Stutz, Nancy Kahn, and Marge Wiener, all of the JFS: Betty Wacksman, Jewish Vocational Service of Cincinnati; the emigrés who filled out our questionnaires and graciously cooperated in allowing us to interview them; the other case workers; the volunteers who have done so much to make the absorption process a success and this study possible. We also thank Professor Susan Kay and her graduate assistant, Pat Dunham, for their technical assistance; and Dottie Pierson for her attention to details. We needed them all. We thank them all.

with individuals who are exceptional in two conspicuous
respects: (1) that they are Jews and have experienced
various levels of discrimination not suffered by members
of other Soviet nationalities; and (2) that they chose
to leave their homeland while other Jews remained. Consequently, any study of such a select group cannot claim
to reach definite conclusions concerning what the unap-
proachable "average Soviet citizen" thinks about life
under the Soviet system. Our objectives necessarily
must be more modest.

Despite these limitations, we felt that a study
of the emigré experience in Cincinnati, Ohio, with its
active Jewish community, presented fascinating possibilities. How would these Russian Jews react to life
in a midwestern, highly suburbanized community? What
expectations would they have of life in America; and
to what extent would reality coincide with these fan-
tasies? Would they experience a sense of cultural dis-
orientation? Would they have difficulties finding jobs
comparable to those they held in the USSR? How would
they evaluate both the American and Soviet systems? And
finally, how would the Cincinnati Jewish community absorb
these Soviet Jews? In the fall of 1978 we began a research project to investigate these questions, a project
which extended over two years and numerous unforeseen
challenges.

I

Jews were among the earliest settlers of Cincinnati.
The first congregation was organized in 1824, making
Cincinnati the oldest Jewish community west of the
Alleghenies; and by the 1850s, it was the third largest
Jewish city in the United States. The origin of its
population was strongly German, as was that of most of
the city's citizenry, especially after the collapse of
the revolution of 1848 in Germany and the subsequent
flight to America. Germans felt a particular affinity
for Cincinnati because the Ohio River at that point,
with hills covered with grapevines rising on either side,
seemed to them to resemble the Rhine.

In the third quarter of the nineteenth century,
Cincinnati became the home of the reform movement in
America. This, added to the Western orientation of the
earlier Jewish population, presented a hostile Jewish
environment to the large numbers of Eastern Europeans
who began arriving in Cincinnati as refugees from the
pogrom of 1881. The German Jewish burghers of Cincinnati
resented the intrusion of the Eastern European, Orthodox

newcomers. A barrier, not unknown elsewhere, but very
strong in Cincinnati, was thrown up between German and
Russian Jews. It was not breached until after World
War II, and still has not been completely dissolved.

Though the Cincinnati Jewish community is an old,
well-established, and prosperous one, it has not developed the tradition of contributing to Jewish causes to
the same extent as many other similarly endowed communities. It has the reputation of being one of the poorer
contributors to Federation drives. When the call first
went out, in the early 1970s, for host cities to volunteer to receive Soviet migrants, Cincinnati was slow
to respond. The first Soviets to reach Cincinnati did
not arrive until mid-1973. But Cincinnati, under the
aegis of the Jewish Family Service (JFS), thereafter
developed a program of excellent quality to service the
needs of the new arrivals.

While it has been repeatedly asserted that the USSR
was closed to emigration after the 1920s, there was,
in almost every year of the ensuing four decades, some
movement of Jews and others out of the country to the
West. For example, in 1968, 231 Jews left the USSR for
the West.

But then suddenly in 1969, 1970, and 1971, the number
of emigrés, primarily Jewish, began to increase markedly,
almost 13,000 Jews obtaining permission to leave in 1971.
The Soviets have never given any satisfactory explanation
as to why they suddenly raised the barricades. It would
seem that there were primarily two reasons: first, to
get rid of what seemed to those in the Kremlin to be
a distasteful, intellectually and professionally aggres-
sive, trouble-making minority; second, to try by means
of appearing to be more cognizant of human rights, to
convince the United States and the West in general that
they should grant the USSR improved trading conditions.
The Soviet Union badly needed Western technology and
capital. Letting a few Jews go seemed a cheap and easy
way to accomplish those objectives.

By 1973, the number of Jews exiting the Soviet Union
reached 33,500. But in that same year Congress made
it clear that it was not about to grant the USSR the
favorable trade terms it hoped for. Consequently, the
number of Jews permitted to leave was reduced. In 1976,
only a few more than 14,000 Jews were allowed to leave
Russia.

While Jews began leaving the Soviet Union in large

numbers in 1969, they did not begin coming to Cincinnati until 1973, when eight arrived. In 1974 and 1975, when the number leaving the Soviet Union was decreasing, the arrivals in Cincinnati increased. In 1977, when emigration from the USSR began to increase again, in Cincinnati it decreased. However, 1979, which was the year for maximum emigration from Russia, was also the year for maximum immigration to Cincinnati, with 163 new arrivals.

Those coming to Cincinnati overwhelmingly have followed the Vienna-Rome-New York route. A few have gone to Israel and then come to Cincinnati. A few more have been elsewhere in the United States--Texas and Oklahoma, for example--before coming to Cincinnati.

Those who have come to Cincinnati confirm what has been reported elsewhere: that if they state their interest in going to Israel, they are flown off to Tel Aviv after a few days. If they want to go to the United States, they have to endure a wait of two to five months in Rome, sometimes longer.

They report no overwhelming pressures either in Vienna or Rome to go to Israel. Interestingly, almost every interviewee feels the necessity of providing an excuse for not having gone there and for having preferred the United States: Israel is for those with religious and Jewish commitments; we have relatives in the United States; the economic opportunities in the United States are better; we are tired of war, which is a constant threat in Israel; our child is ill and medical facilities in the United States are superior, etc., etc.

As for why the Russians have come to Cincinnati, the answer increasingly is because they already have family there. Since 1979, only those with first degree relatives in Cincinnati have been provided with support. Otherwise, the number of settlers would be greater than the community is able or willing to support. In the early 1970s, however, the reason for coming to Cincinnati was most frequently that there happened to be an allotment number open there.

Soviet citizens arriving in the United States are met by a Hebrew Immigrant Aid Society (HIAS) representative and are lodged overnight in a New York City hotel. The next day they are sent on their way to Cincinnati, where they are met by a case worker from the Jewish Family Service, which has received background information on them from HIAS in Rome. Also present at the airport are one or more members of the new Russian community in Cincinnati, and today, almost without exception, relatives who have come to Cincinnati earlier.

At first, the next step for arrivals was to take them by car to the offices of the JFS in Roselawn, a Cincinnati suburb, where there was a small party and a briefing as to what support was available and what, in general, should be expected to happen in the period immediately ahead. Gradually, however, it became apparent that the new arrivals were not prepared for the sparseness of what earlier Russian writers have referred to as "one-story America." They were used to the six, eight, and ten floor buildings in a city center, with streets filled with people, scurrying to get from one shop to another, jostling, pushing, sometimes stopping and talking. By comparison, Roselawn, where the Russians were usually housed, seemed depopulated, almost desolate. It was eerie. After a time, it became customary to make a side-trip on the way back from the airport, stopping off in downtown Cincinnati, preferably at the height of the business day, so that the newcomers could be reassured by seeing tall buildings and crowds. However, even today, among Russians who have been in the city for half-a-dozen years, there are laments about the lack of urban activity and the observation that the street scene in New York is more akin to what they have known in Leningrad, Riga, and Odessa.

After having inspected the downtown area, Roselawn, the JFS office, the next stop is "home." At first this was almost always (two-thirds of the time) in the Swifton Village Apartments, a huge complex holding some 6,000 people, many of whom are members of minorities and on welfare. The accommodations are not choice, being of post-World War II barracks-type construction; they are poorly maintained, though there has recently been some improvement in the latter respect. Today the JFS continues to use the Swifton facility (though not so frequently as earlier) because apartments there are available--Swifton has a rapid turnover--and because they are cheap. By the standards of many eastern cities in the United States, these garden apartments are quite respectable, if not luxurious. The Russians sometimes complain about "conditions" where they have been placed, but they also express satisfaction with the great amount of room they have in Swifton compared with the Soviet Union. Many who could afford to move elsewhere are still there years after they have come to Cincinnati.

When the Russians arrive at their new home, they find it already furnished, from an immense supply of second-hand furniture that has been collected by volunteers and is now stored in a warehouse. Increasingly, previously-arrived family members participate in fixing up the apartment, providing personal touches that will make things seem more kak domoi, as at home.

Sometimes the by-then exhausted and confused newcomers will be left to "sleep it off." But often they are hustled off to see one of the wonders of the New World: the fresh fruit and vegetable department of the nearby Kroger's supermarket. Eyes pop at the mountains of apples, oranges, grapefruits, pineapples, bananas, cherries, plums, peaches, and so forth. Cameras appear and pictures to be sent back to Russia are taken of the new arrivals and their relatives standing in front of the largess of American agriculture.

A few days later, sometimes a week if older people who require rest are involved, the case worker begins to work concentratedly with her new clients. She takes them to a store and teaches them the rhythm of mercantile life in America, which is quite different from that in the USSR. Where applicable, she takes them to social service offices to register them for the benefits which are available to them. She arranges their visit to a clinic, to make certain that they are healthy or that they receive the medical and dental services that so many of them require.

It is only after two to three weeks that the adult members of the immigrating families are taken to the Jewish Vocational Service (JVS). By this time, a few eager beavers have already made visits to the JVS on their own or have located jobs, usually through relatives. But for the most part, the Russians are not yet ready either physically or psychologically to seek employment. It may be months before they are ready--and a few have never made it into the ranks of the employed, either because they have no marketable skills, are elderly, are not interested, or prefer to become housewives.

In the meantime, as they adjust to life in America, they are aided by the services, facilities, and payments made available by the local Jewish community and recently the federal government through the JFS. These include:

a.   A weekly budget of $128 for a family of four (as of May 1, 1980);

b.   A year of free medical and dental care, not including dentures;

c.   A year's membership at the Jewish Community

Center (usually renewable);
    d.   English language classes; and
    e.   A year's tuition for the children of the
family at either of the two local Hebrew day schools
(usually renewable).

II

In an attempt to determine how Cincinnati Jews reacted to the newly arrived emigrés, we approached three
distinct groups that have had varying degrees of contact
with the Russians: the case workers from the JFS and
the JVS; a select group of contributors to Jewish philan-
thropic causes who are the people bearing the brunt
of the financial burden for the resettlement program;
and finally, the volunteers dealing with the individual
families during their first critical months in Cincinnati. We wanted to determine how each of these groups
perceived the motivations of the Russians, and how they
personally evaluated the necessity and the success of
the program.

From the case workers at the JFS, a picture emerged
of idealistic individuals committed to aiding a group
of people who were viewed by them as "emigrés," not
refugees. They did not see themselves as performing
a mission of human salvation akin to the post-World War
II experience; rather they regarded themselves as providing services to people who chose to seek a better
life for their children and greater educational opportunities free from the growing discrimination experienced
by Soviet Jewish youth. To the social workers, the
emigrés were not victims of extreme oppression or individuals primarily motivated by a desire for greater
personal, political, or religious freedom. While they
frequently mentioned the anti-Semitism embedded in Soviet
culture, they were far more likely to view the emigrés
as desirous of attaining greater economic opportunity.

This perception of the emigrés as materialistically
motivated may simply result from the ambivalent attitude
of the emigrés to the social workers. The Russians are
described as vacillating between subservience and an
obvious desire to please the social workers on the one
hand, and a badgering, demanding attitude upon the other.
The early arrivals had great difficulty comprehending
that the JFS is a private organization, not an arm of
government, and they proceeded to bully the social workers
as they had uncooperative Soviet bureaucrats. The three
social workers, consequently, were the recipients of an

onslaught of complaints--about apartments, furniture,
push-button telephones, etc.--most of which emanated
from envy of what other emigrés supposedly had received.
The perception of the Russians as materialistically
motivated was augmented by another factor. The early
arrivals displayed great reluctance to accept jobs that
were even slightly below their positions in the USSR,
this being attributed to their lack of a conception of
job mobility in the United States, having been previously locked in job categories.

When the social workers were asked their assessment
of how the emigrés reacted to American life, the
former's responses reflected the chorus of complaints
to which they had been subjected about the anomie of
suburban life, the lack of strong support "networks"
of friends and family that they had experienced in the
Soviet Union, the superficiality and frivolousness of
Americans, and their preoccupation with television--
all reactions reminiscent of Solzhenitsyn's critique
of American life. The social workers did not hear the
broadly based sentiment among the emigrés we interviewed
who extolled the greater freedom and independence of
American society.

To a great extent the feeling of isolation and up-
rootedness previously indicated was most pronounced among
the early arrivals when contact with other Russians was
minimal, when old ties of friendship were dissolved under
the pressures of a new environment, and class snobberies
prevented any attempts at organizing a support system.
We have seen some indications in talking to the newer
arrivals that as the total number of immigrants has increased, and as relatives of the first arrivals have
come to Cincinnati, some of these problems of alienation
and loneliness have been alleviated. However, the immigration process is still quite distressing for several
age groups, particularly teenagers who had no personal
motivation for leaving their friends and were not dissatisfied with their lives in Russia, and the aged who
came because their adult children had chosen to leave.
It is interesting that the social workers disagreed about
the severity of adjustment among the latter group with
the assessment made by the Russians themselves. All
the Russians with whom we discussed the matter felt that
emigration was most traumatic for the elderly who had
left behind an accustomed existence to confront an alien
culture, the language of which they would have no employment incentive prompting them to learn. The social

workers, however, felt that these elderly people suffered
the fewest adjustment problems, while they saw the
middle-aged, presented with the immediate difficulties
of mastering a new language and finding employment, as
having the most difficult time. This discrepancy can
be attributed to the daily pressures on the social
workers to solve the complaints raised by the most vocal
group of immigrants.

Among these key figures directing the resettlement
program, there was a strong commitment to freedom of
choice for the Russians without any resentment that they
had chosen to come to the United States rather than
Israel. But they did relate what they sensed to be a
fairly pronounced trend in the Jewish community and
particularly among those individuals responsible for
the allocation of charitable funds, that a disproportionate amount of money was being spent on these migrants
who were not really Jews in any meaningful, religious
sense. This resentment was augmented by a negative
evaluation of the Russians as overly demanding, and
desirous only of material advancement, not freedom. We
conducted a series of polls among Jewish contributors
in an attempt to assess the breadth of these complaints,
and our results indicated that these kinds of criticisms
were endorsed only by a very small minority.

Given the intensity of the demands placed upon the
JFS social workers and their tendency to view their role
as that of servicing clients rather than of rescuing
victims of oppression, it is not surprising that the
turnover rate among the paid professionals has been pronounced. All three of the women that we interviewed
in the spring of 1978 who were dealing with the Russians
as case workers left their jobs shortly thereafter,
having experienced acute feelings of exhaustion from
the demands placed upon them by the immigrants. In contrast, the individual in charge of placing the Russians
in jobs at JVC who is not a professional social worker
and who views her job more as aiding victims of oppression, remains enthusiastically at her task.

Having heard rumors from various sources that Jewish
leaders and the community in general were growing skepti-
cal of the diversion of funds away from the established
pattern of Jewish welfare functions to the Russian resettlement effort, we conducted a survey among representative groups of Cincinnati Jews. The first poll
was conducted at the JFS annual meeting in April 1979
where one would expect to find a more aware and know-

ledgable group, one supportive of the resettlement program; the second, in which mail questionnaires were sent
to a random sample of contributors to Jewish philanthropies was conducted in the summer of 1979.[2] In addition to assessing the validity of these rumors concerning
the expenditure of funds to support the Russians, we
wanted to gauge the impact of the emigrés upon the
community.

 Both groups responded identically to a question
inquiring about the balance struck between the needs
of local Jewish services and those of the Russian Jews.
Approximately 8 percent felt that too much money had
been diverted from local needs, while 26 percent felt
that the right balance had been reached. A rather surprising 65 percent responded that they "don't know,"
which indicated a widespread ignorance of the extent
of financial commitment by the Jewish philanthropies.
On the extent of dissatisfaction among Cincinnati Jews
concerning the refusal of these Soviet Jews to settle
in Israel, we found an overwhelming sentiment among both
groups for freedom of choice. Roughly 5 percent of each
group felt that "the donations of Cincinnatians would
do double service if these Russian Jews had gone to
Israel," while 87 percent selected an option that gave
the Russians a choice about whether they would settle
in the United States or Israel. The group that received
the mail questionnaire was presented with an additional
option, one that gave the Russians a choice but would
strongly urge them to go to Israel; 33% of the respondents opted for this answer with 54 percent choosing
the more lenient selection of complete freedom of choice.
Thus, an overwhelming majority of both groups (87%) endorsed freedom of choice. This reaction diverges
markedly from the rumors we had heard. Apparently, the
disaffection of some community leaders does not enjoy
broad support.

 To appraise the involvement of Cincinnati Jews with
the Soviet emigrés, we inquired about the extent of contact the former had experienced with them.[3]

	None	Single Setting Casual Contact	Multiple Casual	Extensive
JFS group	32%	19%	6%	43%
Cincinnati Jews	42%	32%	9%	17%

Among the general population of Jews sampled by mail questionnaire* (with the significant proviso that those who have had contact with the Russians would be more likely to respond), we can conclude that while the Soviet Jews have, considering their small numbers, made their presence felt in the community, there has not been an extensive level of contact. Even among those at the JFS annual meeting, an elite and one would assume concerned group, a rather surprising 32 percent reported having had no personal contact with any Soviet Jews. It is no wonder, then, that the Russians themselves have experienced a sense of isolation.

How did the Americans assess the motivation of the Russians in leaving the Soviet Union? Here, we see significant differences depending upon the extent of contact a person had with the emigrés. Among the general population of Jews the predominant expectation was that the Russians were motivated principally by a desire to escape oppression (48%), or to attain freedom (23%), rather than to gain opportunities for their children (10%), or for economic reasons. The JFS group, however, was less likely to perceive the Russians as motivated by the desire to escape oppression (only 26%). For both groups, the more extensive the contact with Russians, the less likely that the Russians were viewed as desirous of escaping oppression or attaining freedom and the more likely that they were viewed as leaving for the sake of their children or for economic reasons. Thus, a process of disenchantment seemed to occur as the Americans came to know the Russians. They are seen less in stereotypical or ideological terms--as freedom fighters or victims of an oppressive regime--and more as ordinary people with normal motivations. This reaction complements that experienced by the case workers, while it departs from the self-assessment proffered by a significant number of the emigrés.

Interesting, also, is the extent to which a respondent's evaluation of the emigrés' motives influenced the evaluation of the balance of monies being spent between Russian and other community services. For those who saw the Russians as motivated by economic reasons, 45 percent of those who had an opinion felt that too much money had been spent on the Russians. In contrast, among those who viewed them as motivated by the desire to escape oppression or to attain freedom five times

---

*Referred to in these tables as Cincinnati Jews.

as many people selected "right balance" rather than "too
much money."

Members of both United States groups projected a
dire vision of the situation of Jews in the Soviet Union
with 48 percent speculating that Jews were treated much
worse than ordinary Soviet citizens, and 34 percent se-
lecting the even more emphatic choice "persecuted and
worsening." Here, the extent of contact with the
Russians had no effect upon the response, which is
easily explicable because the Russians themselves evaluate the condition of Soviet Jewry in similarly drastic
terms.

The extent of communal awareness of the paucity
of religious training among the emigrés is extremely
high, with 64 percent of the Cincinnati Jews and 82 percent of the JFS group realizing that the Russians have
had no or very little religious training. Political
attitudes of the Russians proved an enigma to the
Americans with only 52 percent of the respondents confident enough to hazard a guess. Of those, substantial
numbers expected Marxist propaganda to have had a substantial effect upon the emigrés, as the following chart
indicates. The Russians themselves, as we shall examine
shortly, seem far less enamored of Marxism or socialism.

Marxist/Communist	14%
Socialist	24%
Liberal	14%
Middle of the Road	14%
Conservative	24%

Among the Cincinnati Jews there was a pronounced
expectation that the Russians would react to American
life with gratitude rather than criticism.

Attitude Towards American Life

	Cincinnati Jews	JFS	All
Grateful	43%	24%	37%
Isolated	14%	31%	19%
Very critical	2%	3%	2%
Nostalgic about Russia	3%	5%	3%
Grateful, isolated nostalgic	27%	19%	24%
Isolated, very critical	6%	10%	5%

The responses displayed in this chart indicate an awareness that the adjustment process will be complicated by feelings of isolation, yet Russians are not expected to become antagnostic to American culture. This assessment will prove fairly accurate when we hear from the emigrés themselves, but with perhaps an undue emphasis is upon gratitude.

The Cincinnati Jews expected that the Russian Jews would be hostile towards the Soviet Union while retaining fond memories of Russia (50%), rather than being hostile and harboring bitter memories of Soviet life (14%), or not hostile but regretful (21%). Virtually no one saw them as potential freedom fighters against the Soviet system in the vein of Cuban refugees (a mere 1%).

Finally, of those respondents among the Cincinnati Jews who had personal contact with the emigrés, 57 percent described them in positive terms, 24 percent neutrally, while 17 percent expressed a negative assessment.

What these surveys demonstrated in a resounding fashion was a widespread support for freedom of choice for the emigrés, a general ignorance of or disagreement with the disputes within the Jewish leadership over the allocation of funds, and an expectation that the Russians would respond gratefully towards American society and hold a mixture of hostility towards the Soviet regime and nostalgia for Russian life. Given the almost universal tendency to picture prospects for Jews in the Soviet Union in abysmal terms, it is curious that respondents were split almost evenly between those who saw the newcomers as refugees (46%) and those who viewed them as immigrants (52%).

Our third group of subjects among the Cincinnati Jewish community was comprised of the volunteers who worked with the newly arrived families. These volunteers were approached for their comments in the spring of 1979; thus some of the families that they assisted were later arrivals than the people we polled in our mail questionnaires sent to Soviet emigrés. One would expect a higher incidence of economic motivation attributed to these late arrivals, especially since JFS instituted a policy of only accepting families with relatives already in the Cincinnati area in the beginning of that year. This expectation was amply borne out, with ten of the eighteen respondents considering the desire for greater economic opportunity or betterment of children's futures as the

principal reason that the Russians had for leaving.
Other frequently cited explanations given by the volunteers were a desire for personal, political, or artistic
freedom (5), family members already in the United States
(4), and discrimination suffered in the Soviet Union (4).
One perceptive volunteer captured the difficulty
Americans have in grasping the motivation of the emigrés.
She approached her family with the question directly--
"For what reason did you leave the Soviet Union?" The
family had arrived from Kiev in late 1978 with one
daughter, another daughter having previously emigrated.

> When confronted with this question directly, my
> family showed a hesitation in answering--as if
> they weren't quite willing to fully discuss the
> answer. We have touched upon the subject before--
> and from what I gather from our [many] discus-
> sions in general, I think [I'd be the first to
> admit that I could be "way off"] they did come
> to a certain degree for material and monetary
> betterment--for a more prosperous life. I think
> they are embarrassed to admit this. However, I
> know that they did not live too badly in Russia.
> (Ed.: the husband was a dispatcher and the wife
> an economist.) Also, we have discussed many
> situations of religious prejudice towards Jews,
> and the limited opportunities of Jews and the
> common man in Russia.

After much animated discussion, the mother finally
announced that they had emigrated solely for the sake
of their daughter, who had been divorced in the United
States and who needed them.

After much frustration with the less than overwhelming response rate to our mail questionnaire to the
Soviets and after speculations about the possible causes
(e.g., Were the Russians afraid of repercussions against
relatives still in Russia despite promises of anonymity?
Were they suspicious of us as possible government spies?
Or were they simply unaccustomed to being polled on any
topic?), we requested that the volunteers approach their
families with our original questionnaire. Again, the
result was exiguous, but we did confirm some of our sus-
picions. Volunteers reported that they simply could not
persuade their families that we were not government in-
formants. From the volunteer previously quoted, the
following trenchant response was submitted:

I'd also like to mention that the idea of these
questionnaires was not at all well received--
they immediately showed resentment and almost
anger--although they seemed to understand why
only between themselves and did not really explain to me. The mother got especially excited
and said, "We've already done that before--long
time ago." I just got the idea that they either
considered it an imposition and/or that they were
"above" this. Maybe it's just a desire to
"assimilate" and not be singled out and "re-"
considered Russian-Americans or immigrants? . . .
A most interesting reaction was from the
[divorced] daughter--who has her own apartment
and has been here three years--she seemed to
think it was silly--not for her. But I can see
how highly she values her Americanism and her
ability to adapt. She has done so, very well.

The volunteers who deal intimately with the emigrés
in the latter's first few months in the United States
were the group of Americans most attuned to the difficulties encountered by the Russians during this critical
adjustment period. Virtually every volunteer emphasized
the language barrier as the principal obstruction to
employment and adjustment to American culture. Without
a grasp of the language, the emigrés experienced isolation and an inability to assimilate. Also, as job appli-
cants the Russians were unaccustomed to interviews and
rejection, and they often felt a loss of esteem when
they were unable to find employment providing exactly
the same social stature that they enjoyed in the Soviet
Union. But language difficulties remained preeminent;
and we suspect from our interviews with Russians who
have been here longer, that once this impediment is con-
quered the other complaints seem to lessen and job satisfaction increases. Many volunteers thought their
families expected immediate success with remuneration
comparable to that of Americans they saw around them.
"They find out very soon what Americans make and expect
to make the same thing. They are not content to wait
for homes, cars, etc., but want everything right away."
It is rather ironic that Solzhenitsyn's acquisitive,
materialistic Americans find precisely the same faults
in these Soviet emigrés.
Throughout our study we were particularly interested
in the expectations that the emigrés had of American life

and the extent to which these had been realized. The
volunteers displayed insight into some of the problems
raised when the emigrés' preconceptions confronted reality. The following responses are representative:

> 1. They expected to be transferred from
> their previous lifestyle to the same lifestyle
> within the first year.
> 2. They had a "story-book" expectation
> of life in America and hoped to have all the
> advantages [car, TV, affluence, modern conveni-
> ences, etc.] in a few short months. It has been
> terribly difficult to satisfy these expectations
> in such a short time.

Professional families were viewed as more realistic in
their assessments and less demanding of immediate material satisfactions, while the less educated constantly
clamored for air conditioners, vacuum cleaners, and
luxuries. Interestingly, the intellectuals and professionals among the Russians we interviewed displayed a
contemptuous attitude toward their countrymen of the
working class precisely because of these acquisitive
characteristics, several suspecting their possession-
dominated brethren of having acquired their proclivities
from activities on the Soviet black market. What emerged
from these interviews was an abiding sense of class differences felt by the Russian intellectual elite, coupled
with embarrassment that their compatriots were giving
all the emigrés a bad reputation with their crass self-
seeking.
The volunteers' reactions to their experience
working with the emigrés varied dramatically and were
highly idiosyncratic; the most interesting of these responses are reproduced below:

> 1. The problem of immigration is intensified
> by the fact that the economic conditions of this
> group of emigrés was, relative to the rest of the
> country, not bad. The identification of a person
> is solely with his work image--there is no other
> outlet. The women, taking longer to employ, be-
> come very depressed without work. I have seen
> little evidence of hobbies or outside interests
> in most families.
> 2. They want to fit into the American culture,
> but they also want to preserve their Russian back-

ground. They are concerned that their young
children will forget the language. They seem to
want to pick out things from our system and yet
preserve their "Russianness." They are extremely
anxious though, to find and make American friends.
I've found them to be very modest--Victorian in
their attitudes about sex education and information, men and women generally don't discuss the
subject in mixed groups.

    3. There is just so much more than meets the
eye. One wants to be able to be of the most help
possible. They seem to like American friends, yet
do not have many. Also, I think they reinforce
one another by their close associations with their
own relatives here in the United States. There
is a need to be more involved with everyday, local
life and lifestyles. I am perplexed! I can't
determine their degree of contentment or resentment
in _general_. We discuss fully _every day affairs_,
good and bad: the jobs, learning to drive, costs
and kinds of food, learning English, where they're
going Saturday, etc. But I don't know if they
will, for example, look back in five or ten years
and say: "What if . . .?" Is the change too great?
Were the sacrifices worth it? Is this the kind
of life they want? Don't they feel caged in? And
do they feel a great sense of freedom, too?

    4. I found that it has been very difficult
for these people to try to accept any part of the
American lifestyle. They have left the USSR by
choice, but are not willing to find much about our
country that is nearly as good as it was in Russia.
Their attitude is totally negative. I feel this
particular problem is not a common one for most
of the emigrés, but more likely a personality problem of the family with whom I've been in contact.

    5. My other major reaction is a feeling of
sadness for many whom I have met. For many, America
has been a great disappointment. Especially those
in their sixties and older who moved here to be
near their children. They do not even try to learn
the language and have often expressed their unhappi-
ness to me. There are some young people I know,
single and in their thirties, who are unhappy too.
They often say that many of them wonder what they
are doing here after all. A lot of the familial
relationships and obligations which they felt in

Russia disappear very quickly here. Families who
once lived several generations together in very
close quarters split up here and maintain weekly
contact at best. Perhaps my observations, which
may seen negative at this point, will change over
the next few years. Most of the people I have
known have been here anywhere from a few months
to a few years. Naturally, their adjustment
during this period is going to be difficult.

On a more optimistic note:

    6. We have found this experience to be very
rewarding. Our family is very loving and appreciative of anything we do for them. They are trying
to teach us about their Russian customs and hope-
fully we will teach them ours. In the month that
they have been here, they are already trying to
"Americanize" themselves by cutting their children's hair short and by buying jeans, etc. I
still think that they will continue to keep their
Russian customs and integrate them into living in
America.
    7. Our families can't get over our American
freedom of movement. One family is trying to see
the U.S. and Canada at a frenetic pace. After the
wife asked me for some specific information about
a trip they wanted to take, I commented on their
travels. G. said, "Harriet, you just can't know
what it's like to suddenly be able to come and go
whenever you want. I keep thinking I will wake
up and this will all be over."

Difficulties in reaching valid generalizations
abound in such a study of a diverse group of individuals,
with different backgrounds, educational levels, and job
skills. Compounding these problems is an additional
complexity borne of the reluctance of most of the
Russians to trust academics enough to respond to questionnaires or consent to interviews. While the remarks
of the volunteers are often unique and highly impression-
istic, they do reflect a host of complaints about
material conditions, and expectations so unrealistic
as to defy ready fulfillment. It is noteworthy that
we did not uncover complaints of this nature among the
highly educated and easily assimilated individuals who
agreed to cooperate with our own investigations by

allowing themselves to be interviewed.

Several generalizations do emerge in reflecting upon
the plethora of information we elicited from the case
workers, the Jewish Community, and the volunteers. The
people confronted with the newly arrived Russians on
a daily basis became easily overwhelmed with the latter's
settlement problems: language impediments, employment
dissatisfactions, and assimilation difficulties. Naturally, this resulted in some individuals abandoning their
initial idealistic vision of themselves as saving victims
of Soviet oppression; and perhaps they overreacted when
they then characterized the emigres as people obsessed
with purely materialistic objectives. This phenomenon
is most conspicuous among the disaffected case workers
and one senses a similar disillusionment among some of
the volunteers.

For the Jewish community of Cincinnati, the support
for the Russians remains fairly strong, with freedom of
choice with respect to settlement in the United States
rather than Israel endorsed by resounding majorities.
Yet, few have had significant personal contact with the
Russians and this is certainly a factor in the adjustment problems experienced by the emigres who sorely miss
the intimate associations and friendships left behind
in their homeland. For them, family and a few intimate
friends that one could trust held an importance in their
lives that few Americans can really comprehend. As
several intellectuals related to us, in the USSR friendship was of supreme importance when your future existence
depended upon the reliability of those to whom secret
thoughts had been confided. In America, where there
is no KGB potentially lurking behind every confidential
conversation, American friendships seem to the Russians
to be all too superficial and banal.

While those among the Jewish community who had the
least contact with the Russians tended to view them as
victims of oppression or as seekers after personal freedom, those intimately connected with their resettlement
held a far less sanguine view of their motivation for
emigrating. For these case workers and volunteers, the
acquisitiveness of the Russians was their most conspicuous attribute. Perhaps the new Soviet man is not a
creature of a different nature from his capitalistic
forebearer, all prophecies of Marxist ideology aside.

III

The remainder of this study focuses upon the
Russians themselves: how do they appraise their experience now, from the perspective of months or, in some
cases, several years in the United States? But before
we permit the emigrés to speak, let us examine their
backgrounds in Russia and the extent to which their
aspirations for a job commensurate with their skills have
come to fruition. For the emigrés, as for their hosts
at the JFS and the JVS, the first crucial hurdle is securing that first position--conquering the interview,
dealing with rejection, and finally, landing the job.
We wondered whether the Russians succeeded in finding
employment comparable to the skills they had acquired in
the USSR. Doubts arose immediately about the method of
classification. Should we rank different occupations by
the status they would hold in the United States or in the
Soviet Union? Were all these Russians who called themselves "engineers" really engineers by American standards? We resolved the former quandry by defining
categories by American standards, thus retaining consistency between the employment figures for the USSR and
those of the U.S. The latter puzzle proved more resis-
tant to facile resolution; and after dilligently
examining the employment background of each person who
designated himself or herself as an engineer, we reached
judgments on each case. Clearly, one individual who
repaired radios in Russia was not a "radio engineer" by
our standards; but in other cases we reached decisions
with far less certainty, such as the "elevator engineer"
who was obviously an educated, erudite fellow. But ele-
vators in America function quite well without the
constant surveillance of an engineer. With this caution-
ary admission, we offer the breakdown on the following
page.
     One category of workers are remarkable by their
total absence. Cincinnati has received no collective or
state farm workers. This is consonant with reports of
the presumed policy of the Soviet government against
permitting Jews in the countryside to depart.
     What our research indicates is that those classified
as professionals and intellectuals in the USSR had the
greatest difficulty in attaining employment commensurate
with their skills (or alleged skills, in some cases).
Among those employed as professionals in the USSR (The
vast majority of these were engineers of some variety;

	Employment USSR	Employment USA
Professional (e.g., doctors, engineers, school teachers, factory managers, medical researchers, economists)	13%	6%
Intelligentsia (e.g., movie critics, makeup artists, college teachers, musicians)	4%	1%
White Collar (e.g., lab technicians, sales managers, salesmen, computer programmers, translators)	13%	12%
Blue Collar (e.g., machinists, beauticians, manicurists, electricians, shoe makers, seamstresses)	30%	21%
Farm Workers	0	0
Students, Young Children, Deceased in U.S.	30%	31%
Retired	8%	9%
Housewives	1%	4%
Part-time in JFS Workshop		3%
Unemployed		2%

we received very few doctors or factory managers.), 43 percent found employment in their field, while 33 percent took white collar jobs (In some cases these were trainee positions in their field of expertise.), and 10 percent accepted blue collar positions.[4] However, it is among the intelligentsia that disappointment, at least statistically, appears most acute. Of course, we are dealing with a small number of individuals in this category (17); but there is a pronounced tendency for intellectuals to fall from their positions of high status, with only 31 percent succeeding in finding employment commensurate with their training. For example, a woman from Moscow who was a critic and editor of children's literature secured an instructorship in a small local college. Far more typical of the problem is the case of a Moscow woman television scriptwriter now working in a clerical position, or a mathematician working as a stock boy. The following vivid description of the plight of a musician by a volunteer certainly presents an extreme case, but it does add human dimension to what would otherwise remain lifeless statistics:

> My one "problem family" consisted of husband and wife, both about forty, and a daughter. The wife was a "dentist" in Russia and brought her instruments with her. The husband plays classical music on the bayan. He existed in the classical music world in Russia; however, in the United States it is 90 percent impossible to exist on the same level with an accordian (bayan). The husband is unable to face this. Although he agreed to audition for restaurant playing jobs and was hired, he refused the jobs, saying it made him nervous to play for people who don't listen to him. He has a history of refusing other jobs because it would "hurt his hands." He has been on assistance for over a year, on CETA and unemployment. The husband is still unable to speak English. (However, his wife commented that in the Ukraine, where they lived, he also didn't speak Ukrainian.)

For white collar workers, too, some slippage in classification was evident, with 41 percent remaining in their category, while 33 percent took less desirable jobs, primarily as factory workers. Factory workers (blue collar) had the easiest path to their first jobs, with 82 percent finding comparable jobs, and with little or no period of unemployment.

What we sensed from frequent conversations with the placement personnel at the JVS was that the type of people who came in 1979 were less skilled, educated, and cultured than the earlier arrivals. While the latter speculation probably has substantial validity, from the records we could not discern any significant cultural and skill difference between the new arrivals and the pre-1979 emigrés. However, it is true that the professionals among the two groups fared quite differently; whereas 50 percent of the pre-1979 professionals found comparable employment, only 30 percent of the 1979 group had so succeeded, at least as of this writing. This probably reflects, in part, the economy's steady decline.

It is worth noting that the assessment given by
the JVS people may have been skewed as a result of the
arrival in late 1979 of numerous manicurists and hair-
dressers from Tashkent, all difficult placements and
rather uncouth by American standards. ("How am I going
to find employment for manicurists with chipped nails,
and beauticians with greasy hair?") Fortunately for
the harried placement personnel, many of the dissatisfied manicurists and their equally displeased husbands
soon departed for New York.

Where substantial differences do emerge between
the pre-1979 group and the 1979 group, is in the cities
from which individuals emigrated. By 1979, Cincinnati
JFS had instituted a policy of only accepting individuals
who had relatives already in the city; thus it is interesting to see which groups tended to reinforce their
numbers by, perhaps, encouraging their relatives to leave
the USSR. However, too much in the way of inferences
cannot be drawn from these figures.

	1973-78	1979	All
Ukraine (small cities towns)	4%	1%	3%
Kiev	20%	20%	20%
Lvov	22%	11%	18%
Odessa	13%	5%	10%
Tashkent	10%	39%	22%
Moscow	12%	2%	8%
Leningrad	10%	12%	11%
Other	9%	14%	8%

The Russian Jews who came to Cincinnati were predominantly urbanized, overwhelmingly from large cities,
but not the highly cosmopolitan cities of Moscow and
Leningrad (19%). And yet, practically all the Russians
we interviewed remarked on the lack of a real urban center with towering buildings where they lived. An entire
major city comprised of suburban sprawl they found quite
remarkable. But so, one might add, would an average
New Yorker.

In comparing the place of birth of the emigrés with
their city of emigration a pronounced trend away from
the countryside, its towns, and smaller cities appears.

	Birth	Place of Emigration
Ukraine (small cities, towns)	25%	3%
Major Ukraine Cities		
Kiev	15%	20%
Odessa	8%	10%
Lvov	9%	18%
Moscow	6%	8%
Leningrad	7%	11%
Tashkent	14%	22%
Other minor cities, acquired territories	16%	8%

A movement away from the Ukrainian countryside and into the major cities of Kiev, Odessa, and Lvov is quite evident, with Moscow, Tashkent, and Leningrad benefiting from a migration of less remarkable proportions, at least among the Cincinnati Russians.

The years of arrival for the emigrés in Cincinnati does not strictly reflect the policy tergiversations of the Soviet authorities, as was pointed out earlier. However, their classification by age at date of arrival does substantiate the inference of scholars of Soviet Jewry concerning the failure of the Jewish population to maintain its numbers, as members of an aging community die in greater numbers than are replenished by births.[5]

Year of Arrival	Number of Individuals Arriving
1973	8
1974	23
1975	45
1976	34
1977	33
1978	100
1979	163
Unknown	3
TOTAL	409

Age at Arrival	Number of Individuals
1 - 6	35
7 - 18	77
19 - 30	68
31 - 50	129
51 - 65	57
66 and over	34
Unknown	9

If our families are representative, government propaganda has been remarkably unsuccessful in its campaign to increase the Soviet birth rate, at least among the Jewish population. For those married couples of child-bearing years who have children (the few instances of childless couples were not included), the average number was 1.35 children per family. Not a single family, even among those from Central Asia, had more than two children.

These Soviet Jews voted with their feet when given the opportunity to leave the USSR. How had they reacted to Cincinnati? Would they again move given the opportunity? We attempted to piece together from the records and memories of the case workers an answer to this question for the pre-1979 group. A significant number of families have left Cincinnati; twenty-three family groups out of ninety-one (some comprised of only a single individual, however) have departed with their fifty-seven members out of a total group of 246 individuals. In the case of the sixteen families for which an explanation for leaving could be ascertained, the dominant motivation was a desire to secure a better job (8). Divorce and remarriage played a role in five cases.

Who were these people who left Cincinnati? Perhaps one could approach this question by comparing the tendency of heads of households of each occupational category to depart from Cincinnati.

While 25 percent of all family groups departed the intelligentsia and white collar families left in greater proportions. New York City and, to a lesser extent, Los Angeles, Chicago, and Detroit attracted these emigrés away from Cincinnati. Families who came from Moscow left Cincinnati in disproportionate numbers, a phenomenon not unexpected, given their professional orientation and their desire for a more cosmopolitan environment.

	Number of Heads of Household Who Left	Total Group	Percent Left
Professional	6	22	27%
Intelligentsia	3	7	43%
White Collar	4	11	36%
Blue Collar	9	40	23%
Retired	2	10	20%
Unknown	1	1	

The Soviet emigrés in Cincinnati are essentially people from large cities with the Ukrainian cities dominating. They have been remarkably successful in taking their first steps towards prosperity in America by securing employment. However, for the intelligentsia and some of the professionals, that first job has often proven a demotion from previous Soviet employment. Having ourselves perceived the great value placed upon class status among the Soviet emigrés, this factor undoubtedly represents a substantial source of dissatisfaction. Despite persistent complaints by members of the Cincinnati Jewish community (No informant confessed to holding this view himself!) that the Russians simply want to be given everything without working for it, we have found virtually no reluctance to accept work among the emigrés. As an interesting aside, those expressing such a view on the emigrés are often refugees from Hitler's concentration camps who have settled in Cincinnati. Apparently they resent the Russians being coddled and provided with services unavilable in their time of refuge.

IV

In the winter of 1978-1979 we sent questionnaires by mail to the Soviet Jews who had arrived in Cincinnati between 1973 and 1978, with the purpose of soliciting their responses to several broad categories of questions: (1) What were their sources of information about the United States and what expectations did they nurture? (2) Why did they leave the USSR and choose to settle in the United States rather than Israel? (3) How did they assess the present condition of Jews in the Soviet Union and their future prospects? (4) How have their political attitudes changed since they arrived, and how do they evaluate American society? and (5) What is their present assessment of the Soviet Union?

Naturally, we were aware of the difficulty of the enterprise, and concerned about the likelihood of an insufficient response from these Russians, who are unused to such polling methods, fearful about trusting strangers on such sensitive matters, and hesitant to endanger the safety of relatives still residing in the USSR. Subjects were invited to respond anonymously if they desired; and the questionnaires were sent in both English and Russian. At the time, 246 Soviet Jews had settled in Cincinnati. According to our best calculations, approximately 135 individuals over the age of sixteen could have received questionnaires.[6] The vagaries of the mail service undoubtedly took their toll; we interviewed several Russians who claimed never to have received either mailing of the material. From these efforts we received thirty-seven responses, later augmented by four more requested by the volunteers from their Russian families. Of those, twenty-one people submitted anonymous responses, some supplemented by explanations indicating concern over possible repercussions against their relatives in Russia. For the twenty hearty souls who identified themselves, there was a pronounced tendency to fall into the professional category of job classifications. This was certainly not unexpected, but it does give a definite slant to the responses.[7] We supplemented these reports with extensive personal interviews conducted with some of the emigrés. But again, we interviewed those who had been identified by the case workers as opinionated, representative of diverse perspectives, and willing to speak with us; and these also were predominantly of the professional class.[8]

Foreign broadcasts played a dramatic role in providing the Soviet Jews with information about the United States, with approximately 75 percent of the respondents citing either the BBC, Radio Liberty (VOA), or Radio Israel as sources of information. Many fewer people cited relatives, Western newspapers and books as sources; hardly any had experienced personal contact with foreigners. Soviet propaganda provoked some to read between the lines and draw inferences at odds with the official line about America. "According to Soviet propaganda," one emigré wrote, "there were either capitalists or beggars in the USA; corruption, murders, and drugs. My mother visited her sister who lived in New York since 1914. Mother came back all delighted about life in America. I did not know what to believe." Rumors, inferences, foreign movies all played a part in shaping a

104

very nebulous, indistinct view of American life for most
of the emigrés. We found this particularly striking;
here were people leaving their lives in the USSR with,
for most of them, extremely vague images of what to expect in the United States. While 54 percent of the
respondents supposed that housing conditions would be
good or better than in the USSR, and 43 percent expected
a more active or interesting social life, fully 50 percent anticipated employment difficulties, while educational opportunities were anticipated positively by only
40 percent of the respondents. Significant, also, is
the fact that many individuals displayed no preconceptions about these factors at all (32% on social life
and 27% on educational opportunities), while most of
the others seemed to have had the flimsiest of visions.
The surprising uncertainty of expectations was substan-
tiated by the remarks of the Russians we interviewed,
who often admitted to having no definable sense of what
American life would be like, or their new lives in this
country. Repeatedly, people expressed their surprise
at discovering that all of the United States was not
New York City with giant skyscrapers and teeming masses.
What we sensed was that these people were escaping from
a life that had become either oppressive, unbearable,
confining, or simply inconvenient. Where they were
going appeared to be of less concern than what they were
escaping from. One engineer from Odessa, while more
extreme than most, displayed this sentiment precisely
when he wrote:

> I didn't care what life would be like in the United
> States. I would have gone any place; I was ready
> to die. I didn't leave for the good life. I had
> a high position, special medical care, special food,
> and five times the average income. The matter was
> freedom. I wasn't sure I would get psychological
> freedom. I'm on the way, now, losing some re-
> straints. It will be evolutionary.

While his emphasis upon freedom reflects the impetus
of some of the emigrés, it was certainly more pronounced
in his case, but his comment does reflect a broadly based
desire for escape rather than an affirmative pursuit
of a new life with definable attributes.
Given the imprecision of their expectations, why
did they leave? Of the respondents who chose a single
explanation (The questions requested their principal

motivation), 48 percent cited the prospects of a better
life for their children, 38 percent chose personal or
political freedom, while desire for economic opportunity
garnered a mere 4 percent. Those who selected a variety
of responses displayed a similar breakdown between desire
for freedom and the more prosaic concerns for family
and economic-educational advancement. Many, of course,
came primarily because of the insistence of a vocal,
highly motivated family member.

In our conversations with our select group of
emigrés, the following sentiment occurred repeatedly:

> One part of me didn't work at all in Russia; I
> couldn't talk about what I wanted, or get what
> I wanted. I wanted to be a free person.

Perhaps the most interesting reflection came from an
engineer who had engaged in dissident activities:

> I left because I hated everything--the whole
> system--and customs. The main reason was this--
> if you're a thinking person, and want to know
> the truth, then to be a human being, honest,
> you have not many choices. You can (1) fight
> against the system, which leads to jail or
> the camps; (2) you can play two roles, one in
> public and the other before friends; (3) you
> can stop being a thinking person; or (4) you
> can leave. Most take the second choice. This
> is a highly pressurized life. Every thinking
> person is a potential schizophrenic from the
> pressure of leading a double life.

It appears, then, that the Russians view themselves as
motivated more by concerns for freedom than the Cincinnati Jews realize. Furthermore, what appears to
Americans to be crass materialism on the part of the
Russians is, rather, from their perspective, a concern
to achieve a better life for their children.

In contrast, the Cincinnati Jews accurately portrayed the emigrés as bereft of training in Judaism.
Fifty-six percent reported no religious training and
32 percent had some (but not a lot) of exposure from
relatives; less than 5 percent had any exposure to a
rabbi. What, then, did being a Jew mean to these Soviet
citizens, practically all of whom had Jew as their official nationality stamped upon their internal passports?

For approximately half of the respondents it meant something negative: either feeling like an outcast (38%)
or feeling inferior (11%). But a surprising 33 percent
felt proud to be Jewish. A few expressed ambivalent
reactions of both pride and either inferiority or
alienation.

When requested to describe "the conditions of Jews
in the Soviet Union," 68 percent chose either "much worse
than the average" or "persecuted," in contrast to a mere
22 percent who selected "no difference than the average Soviet
citizen" or only "slightly worse." The proportion of
negative responses was even more pronounced when we inquired about the direction of change towards Jews in
the recent period and the prospects for the future for
Jews in respect to religious freedom, and educational
and job prospects. In response to all these questions,
well over 80 percent felt that affairs had already
gotten worse, either much worse (over 50%) or slightly
worse (over 30%) and that in the specific areas mentioned they would continue to get worse (again, with
the same breakdown between much and slightly worse).

A sense of alienation from Soviet society because
of Jewishness appears to be a prevalent reaction. Only
18 percent felt that ordinary Soviet citizens were
tolerant towards Jews and treated them the same as everyone else. The rest sensed varying degrees of antipathy,
from hostility to extreme hatred or the milder feeling
of being treated as an outsider. One woman expressed
her apprehension of insidious anti-Semitism in these
words:

> Although we have a lot of mixed marriages, Soviets
> and Jews seldom mix. Jews have their own circle
> of friends, Russians their own, where they
> [Russians] express openly their hostility towards
> Jews. In public they seldom attack openly, but
> I felt their hostility constantly.

For others, the discrimination against Jews was more
blatant, as we learned from several of those we interviewed, who related their experiences in gaining admission to universities and higher technical schools. After
passing objective written exams, they were evaluated
poorly on the oral portion and consequently, rejected.
They attributed this to official anti-Semitism. After
retaking entry exams, in some cases three or four times,
they finally secured admission. Several individuals

explained to us that they had chosen mathematics or
engineering precisely because they were fields where
Jews were not prevented from succeeding, since mathema-
ticians and engineers were badly needed.

From the responses elicited concerning their selection of the United States rather than Israel, no easy
generalizations emerge. Given their lack of training
in the Jewish religion, customs, and heritage, their
choice appears unremarkable. Twenty-five percent did
not wish to live in another socialist country, while
12 percent cited greater economic opportunities in the
United States, and a similar number came to be near
relatives. When we asked our interviewees whether they
would have left the Soviet Union if they had Israel as
their only option, everyone answered affirmatively.
Again, this reinforces our impression of their emigration
as a flight from the Soviet Union rather than as a pursuit of a definable ideal.

Assessing the political attitudes of the emigrés
proved difficult. Most, as we discovered during our
interviews, had not thought deeply about politics while
in the USSR. As several people said, what possible point
could political discussions have had when nothing could
be changed, anyway? We observed a tendency among them
to view the Soviet system as monolithic, immutable, and
impervious to analysis. The Russians exhibited an all-
or-nothing attitude towards the system; either it would
last forever unchanged, or it would fall (which no one
thought of as a real possibility), but it would not be
altered by piecemeal reform. The following charts display the political labels chosen by the mail questionnaire respondents:

Political Attitudes in USSR		Political Attitudes in US	
Soviet/Communist	5%	Liberal	43%
Western Democratic	55%	Middle of the Road	10%
Admired Pre-revolution- ary Russian System	5%	Conservative	23%
		Don't Know	18%
Non-Political	33%	Other	6%
Other	2%		

The figures regarding political attitudes once the
emigrés have lived in the United States are particularly
suspect. Those interviewed were found to have scant
awareness of what these categories mean to Americans.
Our strategy with the interviewees was not to ask for a

self-designation, but to propose various policy positions to them for their evaluation. Then, we categorized
them. While these results are fragmentary, no one pro-
fessed consonant with communism, although we did uncover
a smattering of democratic socialists.

But how did these people, raised under the prism of
Soviet propaganda, evaluate American culture and values?
First, how did reality coincide with their expectations?
Responses tended toward the idiosyncratic, but 47 percent
did find life in the United States either better than
or the same as they expected. Others cited a host of
concerns from social problems (crime, race relations,
inflation, permissiveness) to personal economic difficulties. Others found us a boring, uncultured people.
Two of the more thoughtful responses follow: the first
from a middle-aged medical technologist, and the second
from a precocious seventeen year old:

> It is better than I expected. It is real. It is
> life. It is difficult: learning how to drive,
> getting a job, dealing with people; but it is much
> better economically, to begin with, also I am free
> to go from one city to another without asking
> government's permission. I am reading books of
> Soviet writers which I would have never been able
> to read in Russia. I see films of Italian and
> French producers which in Russia were mostly privi-
> leges of the so-called "eleta." There are no
> beggars on the street, at least in Cincinnati.
> But crime rate is even worse than Russian propa-
> gandizing.

> Of course my view of America has changed. It's
> not as idealistic, in many ways, and not as
> polarized. I had a wild image of it: cowboys,
> farms, skyscrapers, heroin on every street corner,
> Ray Bradbury's picture of Midwest from Dandelion
> Wine, you know: mellow, small towns, milk,
> healthiness, fields, cigar store Indians. All
> that stuff is gone. America is more usual, more
> understandable, trivial, more routine. Still
> very neat, though.

Freedom and economic opportunity were the aspects
of American life most often cited approvingly (by well
over 65 percent of the respondents). Responses varied
much more over what disappointed them most about American

life: while 20 percent cited personal economic problems,
others frequently mentioned complaints, including our
low level of culture, medical costs, and too liberal
social mores (11% each). A few of the more provocative
criticisms are worthy of inclusion:

> 1. The desire of Americans to achieve an abso-
> lute personal freedom. Too much weakening of our
> own government. Mild treatment of murderers, outlaws,
> rapists. Disappointing patriotism. No existing
> laws on gun control. No nobility in sacrificing
> material life for defending achieved freedom.
> 2. That so many people, especially intellec-
> tuals, still have some admiration of socialist and
> communist ideas.
> 3. There still is anti-Semitism in America.
> A lot of middle class Americans have an image about
> Jews being greedy, not very smart, and generally
> unclean. It is disappointing, but now I do not
> care about their likes and dislikes. The cultural
> level of middle-class Americans leaves much to de-
> sire. You want to talk about new books, interesting
> movies, discuss an article in the paper, but all
> they are interested in is soap operas and basket-
> ball. I am disappointed by system of school edu-
> cation in America. Teachers do not care whether
> students learn something or not. Also, crime rate
> is high. I am afraid even to drive at night.
> 4. Ugliness of cities. Shallowness of people.
> Our own purposeless situation. A sense of confu-
> sion. Polyester clothes, especially pants--what
> unheard of ugliness!!!

If one can test a person's level of satisfaction
in the negative, then the vast majority of emigrés are
contented, at least to the extent that they do not want
to return to the USSR. Seventy-two percent said they
would not return under any conceivable circumstances,
21 percent might return if communism were overthrown,
but no one displayed a desire to return and live per-
manently in the Soviet Union, under the present regime.
Perhaps a more refined barometer of their own contentment emerges from a question inquiring about whether
they would encourage other Soviet Jews to come to the
United States: 22.5 percent chose the unqualified
selection "enthusiastically encourage," while a resounding 75 percent chose either "yes, but with some reserva-

110

tions," or "depends on particular circumstances." Only 2.5 percent said "no." Some of this hesitancy undoubtedly revolves around the difficulties experienced by the elderly and certain artists, scholars, and musicians. Extracts from a letter smuggled into the Soviet Union by one of the emigrés expresses reservations we repeatedly encountered. After recounting the difficulties experienced by those who will be without a profession here, "bookkeepers, planners, economists, attorneys, dentists, and instructors," the licensing requirements for doctors, the lack of work for classical musicians, and the necessity for writers and artists who are not famous to work at menial jobs, the author continues:

> Of course, it is better and easier to live here. However, whatever we had before, cannot and will not happen here. Before we had enough money for food only and we did not have fear to be without work. Here, on the other hand, as long as you work you have money for everything, yet it is quite easy to lose the job, because everyone lives according to the demand of the market. If there is not demand--the firms are going bankrupt and they close doors. An unemployed can be a laborer, engineer, or president of a firm. Thus, unexpectedly, the firm where I was doing technical translations went bankrupt. Thus 900 dollars that I earned, I will never receive. In short--what the departing persons must know . . . I do not advise categorically to come here the people who are well established and for whom this is the "main thing" in life. The revenge lovers will find failures and disappointments only. Those must come who are deprived of the possibility to do what they like, be it literature, painting, religion, philosophy. Those must come who think of preservation of their spirit over material goods. Those must come who have children and think of them. Children of any parents, in any case will be happy--they will be different. In keeping with these thoughts everyone must come. This dilemma must be resolved by the person himself.

What would the emigrés like to tell Americans about the Soviet Union? Here, the predominant response (55%) was to warn Americans that the Soviet Union was a cruel and oppressive regime, or that it represented a threat

to world peace. Others spoke of the beauty, culture,
and generosity of the Russian people as distinct from
their rulers. Approximately 10 percent of the respondents had positive remarks about the USSR. A sampling
of the range of declarations follows:

    1. Don't hate Russians! It's not their fault;
they are suffering under communist control, too.
One day when communism will be overthrown, Russia
will become a great country, a rich one, free and
happy. But today be aware. Dying shark still can
bite you.
    2. Don't be afraid! Be careful! A frightful
system which corrupts. Frightful rulers and co-
horts. Slaves and robots of ideology. "Die today
so that I can live tomorrow"--their slogan. They'll
do anything to survive. Do not believe any of their
words.
    3. Visit Soviet Union if you have money and
time. It is beautiful old country--Russia, with
cities like museums, with old churches and wide
streets. Visit south of Russia, go to Baltic
cities, to Siberia--it is impossible to describe
the beauty of Russia. But do not talk to people;
they are afraid to talk to you and if they would
talk they will not tell you the truth. Help Jewish
people--do not support Olympic games in 1980 until
they let every Jew who wants out a freedom to go.
They need your help in Soviet Union.

CONCLUSION

    The people we polled and interviewed were not
famous dissidents nor, except in rare cases, even anomy-
mous dissidents,[9] but rather ordinary Soviet Jews; and
what they describe portends a dismal future for Jews
in the Soviet Union. Even beyond that, those interviewed
contended that daily life for everyone in the Soviet
Union had worsened in recent years. While this may represent a psychological overreaction--I left, therefore
everything must have been terrible over there--all those
confronted by our incredulity at their dismal assessment of material conditions in the USSR contended that
their newly arrived relatives all told horror stories
of formerly available goods now vanished, and even
longer and less fruitful queues. The turning point for
Jews in Russia, according to the emigrés, occurred after

the Six Day War in the Middle East. For older folks,
whatever the truth was, the 1930s represented a halcyon
era in which official condemnation and reprisals faced
those fomenting hatred against Jews. Today, in contrast,
many feel that anti-Semitism breeds with official en-
couragement.

To the emigrés who have settled in Cincinnati, the
determination required to leave the USSR seems generally to have been worth the effort. Most seem remarkably well adjusted after being here for a year or more,
though in some cases doubts may have been masked from
us. We anticipated much deeper cultural shock, as though
the mind conditioned by communist education and propaganda would suffer a crisis of disproven facts; but
apparently the degree of skepticism among the emigrés
about anything connected with the system ran so deep
that they were prepared to have Soviet-instilled beliefs
disconfirmed. The middle-aged generation had all sensed
sometime in early adulthood that something was very wrong
with the Soviet system, and that life elsewhere did not
consist of daily struggles for the most basic ingredients
of survival. While they did not know what to expect
in America, they did know that it had to be better, and
more free.

What surprised most of the emigrés about America
appeared to us rather mundane. Most people did not draw
penetrating insights, but rather remarked on the plethora
of goods, the absence of people in the streets, the
suburban sprawl of a midwestern city, and the friendliness of strangers. This reaction surprised us, but
perhaps it should not have. Maybe in a way we, too,
had unconsciously accepted Marx's prophecy that communism
would create a new breed of men. They responded in a
very human, normal way to the immediate details of everyday life. Perhaps, what we expected appeared as the
exception rather than the general reaction. For example,
one woman told us that she was watching the "Tonight
Show" about a month after she arrived and Johnny Carson
told a joke critical of President Carter. She immediately became apprehensive. The next night she tuned
in and Johnny did not appear. She was certain that he
had been arrested, until an American acquaintance explained to her the American concept: "guest host."

Perhaps what is most lamentable, considering the
high degree of support for the resettlement program among
Cincinnati Jews, remains the failure of efforts to reach
out to the newcomers and mingle with them. The

volunteers provide a vital and commendable function,
but the psychological needs of the emigrés require more
than "official" companionship. The sense of isolation
experienced by many, compounded by the class consciousness which separates the emigrés among themselves, is
sad to observe. This isolation was expressed vividly
in the aforementioned smuggled letter:

> . . . Our fortunes do not upset Americans. With
> pleasure they will invite you to their house, they
> will visit you, they know how to drive and eat,
> they chat about weather, sport, seldom about art,
> never about books, and they are always smiling.
> You cannot share with them your problems, doubts,
> or troubles. The relations with Americans can be
> entertaining and friendly only. They will not
> understand nor will they help. They will not
> understand because they feel that everyone has
> his share of problems and why should he have some-
> one else's problems. They will not help because
> their worries are directed to their families.
> Needless to say, there are exceptions. Three
> American families became our close friends.

The Jewish Family Service and the Jewish Vocational
Service have accomplished a remarkable success in finding
housing, education, and employment for the Soviet Jews,
but what the newly arrived seem to miss most is a loss
of communal association and intimacy. One suspects that
this isolation will be relieved over time, and it has
already been ameliorated for some families by the arrival
of relatives. Perhaps their loneliness reflects a funda-
mental difference between suburban life in America and
Russian city life with its intimate gatherings of friends
over a bottle of vodka discussing art, music, ballet,
and the travails of existence. All the Russians we met
dearly loved to converse; but they are probably quite
perceptive in noting a more prosaic patter among
Americans who, in Cincinnati, wax most enthusiastic about
the prospects of the Reds and Bengals, rather than the
fate of the cosmos.

NOTES

1. Our conversations with recent emigrés indicate
that the waiting period between the application for a
visa and one's departure has been considerably reduced

114

to a two-month period. These people were typically aware that they would lose their jobs, and some of them quit in anticipation of leaving.

2. At JFS meeting 120 responses were received from the audience. Our mail questionnaire was sent to a random sample of 925 Jewish contributors to the Jewish Federation. This was the most complete list that any of the Jewish organizations were willing to provide. Again, this is a select group among the total Jewish population of the city, but a particularly important subgroup for our purpose of testing the financial support for the resettlement program. Three hundred responses were received.

3. "Single setting casual contact" includes either (1) casual contact in business establishments; (2) casual social meetings; (3) casual meetings in synagogue. "Multiple casual" comprises a combination of responses (1), (2), and (3). "Extensive" includes knowledge of Russians on a personal, friendly basis.

4. Unemployment (6%), housewife (2%) and retirement, unknowns account for the remainder.

5. See: A. Nove and J. A. Newth, "The Jewish Population: Demographic Trends and Occupational Patterns," The Jews in Soviet Russia Since 1917 (Oxford: Oxford University Press, 1978).

6. We arrived at this figure by eliminating those individuals who had departed Cincinnati, died, or were otherwise unreachable. This represents a 30 percent return rate; not inconsiderable, given the circumstances.

7. Professional - 12; Intelligentsia - 1; White Collar - 3; Blue Collar - 6; Student - 1.

8. Fifteen individuals have been interviewed to date. In the near future we intend to broaden our contacts by interviewing a sampling of individuals from the blue and white collar categories.

9. Only 12.5 percent reported engaging in dissident activities, and even this figure must be hugely inflated as a result of the type of people who cooperated with our study.

Part II
Individual Reactions:
The Emigré Experience

The first two chapters in this section seem to the editors to be particularly fascinating because they describe two perceptions, one by an American and the other by a Russian of their first meeting in Moscow in 1977, the subsequent emigration of the Russian, and his adjustment to the American experience.

The conversations in the third chapter are highlights from interviews conducted with twenty Russian Jewish emigrés during 1979 and early 1980.

In all applicable cases, the names of individuals have been changed for reasons which need no explanation.

5

An Improbable Meeting:
A Lasting Friendship

Joseph Drew

He sauntered over to me unobtrusively.
"Are you here with this exhibit?"
"Yes, I am."
"I see. Then you're an American Jew?"
"Yes."
"Are you in the publishing field?"
"No. I'm a social scientist interested in the cul-
tural aspects of Soviet Jewish life."
"I see. Would you like to talk a bit?"
"Sure."
"Let's go for a walk."
In Russia you learn the rule quickly: if you have
something sensitive to say, you always walk while you
talk.
He wasted no time.
"My name is Alexander Dranov. I am a Soviet Jew,
a professional interpreter and translator. I came here
today because I am anxious to talk to American Jews."
"And I am pleased to meet you. I've come here
hoping to talk with some Soviet Jews about life in this
country."
A young man of thirty-two or so, this fellow had
come upon me when I wasn't really expecting it. Here
we were in the first day of our exhibition. Although
it had not been announced to the Soviet people that a
Jewish books booth was one of the hundreds to be erected
at the giant fairgrounds in Moscow, our exhibition was
already making world history. For the very first time,
American Jews were allowed to sit at a booth in Russia,
stocked with several hundred authentic Jewish books,
available to talk to anyone who happened by. At least
four police heavies, government observers, guarded the
booth; but that was hardly a surprise, and the press of

118

many nations came by frequently to inquire <u>sotto voce</u>
about our progress. Yet, that any Russian Jew would
dare propose openly what this young man was now about
to do was as surprising as all the rest.

"Look here, how would you like to come to my house
for dinner tonight?"

"I'd love to."

"Do you know Moscow?"

"Well, I know the subway map a bit. I tried to
memorize the key points on it when I came to town this
weekend."

"Then do you know Pushkinskaya Station?"

"Yes."

"Can you be there at, say, six tonight?"

"Yes."

"Okay. See you there tonight."

"I'll be waiting."

Unheard of! All the books tell you that you cannot
ever expect to be invited to the home of a Russian. The
Soviet system practically forbids contact with foreigners.
Moreover, the Russians are afraid to invite foreigners
to their homes because most foreigners are tailed by
the KGB. Since the Jewish banks, people were clearly
becoming instant celebrities around Moscow, however,
the opportunity presented by our presence might be sufficient to overcome a more judicious caution. In addition,
the fair was being held pursuant to the terms of the
Helsinki Accords, and our Jewish books booth was part
of the bargain negotiated with the Soviets by the Association of American Publishers. The danger of serious
trouble, for my newly acquired Russian friend or for
our booth's credibility, seemed minimal.

That evening, I excused myself from the booth early.

Although my geographical sense is not bad, I have
never been able to remember faces at all. There I was.
It was six o'clock sharp, and I was standing at the
Pushkinskaya Subway Station platform. But just exactly
what did my young friend look like? I had met so many
people that day, and I wasn't sure. There was someone
who looked like him, standing quietly by a pillar in
the middle of the platform. Was it Mr. Dranov?

A train pulled into the station, heading north.
The young man who I thought was my host-to-be stepped
into it. I did too, retaining enough caution to get
in at the other end of the same car. We rattled along
for a number of stops, and he walked out. So did I.
He turned right, up some stairs, and then emerged into

the fading daylight, stage left. So did I. He waited
at the crowded bus stop above the station. So did I.

A bus painted like all the others pulled into the
stop. It was No. 3. The man I was "tailing" stepped
in at the back of the crowded bus. I plowed into the
middle of it.

Ten minutes later, he got off. I followed. I could
not keep my mind from mulling over the obvious.

Is this my friend, or is the fellow I was supposed
to meet still back there at the original platform in
Pushkinskaya Station? Suppose I am following some total
stranger. Or, suppose that he's the man, all right,
and suppose I am being followed. Maybe I'll lead him
straight into big trouble with the authorities. After
all, we Americans are expected to know all about these
things, and it is possible that Soviet citizens themselves know little about methods of terror in their own
country.

My thoughts were soon jolted by the action of the
man I was tailing. He alighted, and I followed suit.
Within minutes I was walking down a major boulevard in
the Moscow suburbs. He ducked into a booth and then
I heard his voice. "That's fine, fellow, now just turn
to the right at the next corner."

At least I knew now that I was on the right track.
I was indeed following Mr. Dranov.

We soon came astride a large, nondescript building.
We briskly headed into it, climbing up three flights
of stairs in silence. We looked out a window at the
landing, peering left and right.

"It's okay. No one is following us."

"Thank God I found you back there at the subway
station."

"Let's talk later. Right now I just want to give
you the final set of instructions. I live right over
there, in that large building across the way."

How intelligent this man was. He had taken us into
another building first. I could see that I was the real
novice; this Russian man knew how to be sneaky.

"After we cross to the fuilding we will go up
several flights of stairs. Please talk to no one. Just
keep quiet. Now, when we get to the apartment my wife
will open the door. One more thing--about my wife. She's
very frightened over all this, so please be gentle with
her.

"Good. Let's go."

We descended the stairs and quickly moved across a

grey, big city courtyard not unlike my grandfather's
in New York.

Up the stairs. Knock on the door.

As predicted, a woman opened it. She was very
attractive and she was smiling.

"Won't you please come in?" she said in English.

"Thank you," I responded. "I am pleased to meet
you."

"Don't say anything yet, please, Mr. Drew. Wait
one minute," Mr. Dranov said. "Klara, please get me
the blanket."

My young James Bond went over to the telephone.
He took a pencil and twisted the dial midway around its
circuit, jamming the fall backwards with the pencil.
Then he took the large blanket his wife had brought and
he covered the telephone many times.

"Now we can talk," he said finally.

What a world there was to discuss!

As I sat there that night, I kept thinking that
I had fallen into an intellectual gold mine. Here was
a very intelligent man who happened to speak perfect
English. He was an interpreter and an editor, a connois-
seur of Shakespeare and knowledgeable in politics. His
wife had studied English at her college, although she
did not speak the language as well as Mr. Dranov did
and was even less willing to attempt the language beyond
polite phrases. She concentrated, instead, on preparing
dinner.

We talked for several hours that night. I talked
about my life, my jobs, my career plans, and my personal
life. I talked about America, about Israel, about
freedom and democracy. He talked about the miserable
life of Russian Jews, about his own hopes, and about
his family's history. He soon divulged one aspiration,
the explanation for his bold approach to me at the fair.
He wanted to leave for another land, although he was
afraid to apply for an exit visa; his ultimate homeland,
he hoped would be America.

"You know, my mother just called up. She thinks
that I am a complete fool to invite you over. It's so
dangerous, she says, especially if we want to follow
through on our plan to leave this country. Of course,
we can't apply just now; my grandmother is sick. But
we will want to leave sometime in the future, and my
mother is afraid that this will mess up the whole thing."

"Don't worry. I'll try to be discrete leaving tonight and I won't mention our meeting to anyone."

"No, no. I'll drive you back. I've got a car."

The trip back to the hotel--I got out a few blocks from the building itself--was uneventful. I returned with plenty to think about that night.

The next day, Mr. Dranov appeared again at the booth.

"Listen, Joe, tomorrow night is my wife's birthday. We are having a little get-together with some friends. Would you like to join us?"

"Sure. I'd love to."

Once again, the agreement was struck to meet in a subway station. This time, however, the station was closer to his home. I would be more confident of my abilities en route, we decided, and it would be safer that way.

I arrived one hour late, held up by a man at the book booth who kept trying to convince me to embark on some illegal schemes.

There was Mr. Dranov waiting for me.

We got to his house in record time, stopping only to purchase a bottle of champagne for the birthday party. Once inside, we again fixed up the telephone appropriately. This time there were more people to talk to; Sasha--as I was now instructed to call Mr. Dranov-- and his lovely wife, Klara, the birthday girl, had been joined by a number of friends and relatives. Apparently, Klara and I were to share honors for attention that night.

I first noticed and was introduced to a most attractive and obviously gracious lady; it was Sasha's mother, Mrs. Rosa Kurts Dranov. Then I was introduced to another married couple; the man was a business executive named Yuri and the wife was a dentist, Zoya, Klara's cousin. Other friends and relatives were present, including one who had an ex-spouse living abroad.

In my briefcase I carried a tape recorder, among other items. Sasha's mother had been an actress of renown on the Yiddish stage which had flourished in Russia during the thirties; she was probably one of the very few who managed to avoid being arrested and sent to Siberia during the late forties, as Stalin's anti-Semitism began to get the better of him. I asked if Mrs. Dranov would be willing to consent to an interview. I could ask the questions in English and Sasha could translate into Russian. Mrs. Dranov spoke Yiddish, obviously, but I was too weak in that language to carry on a decent discussion.

Much to the surprise of other family members present, Mrs. Dranov agreed to the interview. She was
terribly foolish to do so, according to everyone. I
had been told by the tremendously cautious staff at the
American embassy in Moscow that the Russian guards would
be sure to inspect my bags when I left the country.
(They didn't.) Any suspicious materials would be sure
to receive a special check. I passed this advice from
the embassy along to the Dranov family. Nonetheless,
Sasha encouraged his mother to take the plunge. Here
was a brave family.

I began: "Why was the Yiddish theatre . . . umm
. . . perhaps you could tell me something about the
Yiddish theatre in Russia prior to 1948, maybe before
Mikhoels was killed."

The mother stuttered slightly but soon the interview was on in earnest. Years of persecution, murder,
destruction of the last remaining organs of Jewish culture in Russia came to life, tumbling out of her
recollections.

The interview concluded, we got down to eating the
birthday dinner. Soon, however, the questions resumed.
This time, however, I was to be put on the spot.

"We want to leave Russia," Yuri, the executive,
announced. "We are ready to go now, unlike Sasha, and
we have been thinking about going to Australia. What
do you think about Australia?"

I answered to the best of my ability, trying to
keep my American patriotism from interfering with my
analysis of what life would be like down under. I
managed to do both, I think, putting in a couple of plugs
for the U.S.

"What is crime like in America? What are relations
between the races like? How hard would it be for me
to get a job? Should I go only to New York if I move
to America? How much money do they make? Why do you
not go into business?"

Then Sasha joined in, asking about standards of
living. He knocked me down with his introduction.

"Joe, we want to move to America because we want
to gain our human rights. But let's face it. We know
that we will be taking an economic cut in so doing."

"What in the world are you talking about?"

"Well, look here. Look around you. You know, I
am considered practically bourgeois in this building.
I've got two rooms and a kitchen and a bathroom, and
there's only the three of us--Klara, the child and myself.

Also I have a car. Do you know how rare all this is?"

Sasha had the car because he had once been sent off to Burma as an interpreter. The money he had made abroad while on official mission had gone into the car, as I understood it.

"Sasha, I guarantee that the American family of average means lives better than you in terms of material possessions."

"Really? Come on, now."

"It's true."

I looked around the apartment. The few material possessions he had were relatively uninspiring. The food we were eating was virtually inedible to me, although Klara's ability in the kitchen had disguised that fact somewhat. The living room doubled as a bedroom. It was also serving as the dining room at that moment. The apartment was serenaded intermittently by the screech of a railroad train moving by every so often, and the whole place had a dingy feeling to it. At least so I thought.

I concluded the dinner with what I had conjured up to be a rousing lecture on the nature of freedom and democracy. In retrospect, it might not have been. I pointed out that the delegates to the book fair had just heard the mayor of Moscow welcome them to the city. The speech was as uninspiring as it was vapid. Nonetheless, the audience applauded at the end. I compared that speech with one I had heard the mayor of New York give a week earlier; it had been broadcast over television. In the midst of a tough re-election campaign, the mayor was being heckled unmercifully when I turned on the TV. The dramatic highlight of the speech came when his face was selected as the receptacle for a pie. There you've got it, I said.

"We have freedom and democracy. You've got slavery. But in some respects, our society is losing the old, internalized values which turned us into the greatest colossus in the world. You've got the dictatorship of a small elite. But, presumably, your politicians don't get pies thrown in their faces. You have order, that old nemesis of freedom."

"I'll take my way anytime, but you have to choose on your own. And if you opt to come to the United States, you'll be most welcome. But you will have to learn to adjust and to make your own choices in life."

I met with Sasha and his family one more time. It was several days later. First we went to the house of

an elderly man who wanted help in publishing material
in the West. Near the end of our evening at his home,
Sasha's mother asked that I provide an important service
for her. Would I please find out what was printed in
the West about her father?

I asked for all the details. He had been a prominent actor on the Yiddish stage; Mr. Kurts had played
in houses all across Eastern Europe, in fact. By a
stroke of bad luck, he was trapped in Warsaw during the
war and confined to the Ghetto. As far as she knew,
he had been killed by the Nazis. She did know for sure
that there was an article about her father in a publication. The title of it was Lexicon. My job was to
find that article and send it to her.

Of course, I said I would try. "But it will be
difficult. The word 'lexicon' in English means almost
the same thing as dictionary. There will probably be
hundreds of books with that word in the title. But
I'll try."

Sasha then said that finding that article could
be the most important thing I would ever do for him.
Why? It was vital for several reasons, of which the
most significant was that he couldn't get any information
about the grandfather or his death in Russia. The communist regime doesn't tolerate any books on Jewish resistance and heroism in the Warsaw Ghetto, and even the
word "holocaust" as applied to the death of the Jews
in World War II is unknown to Soviet Jewry. Yet, Sasha
would probably need that information on his grandfather
in order to obtain permission to leave from Soviet officials. Unless he could prove that the old man was dead,
he might be asked to obtain the grandfather's signature
on his application forms. And this he couldn't offer,
unless I sent the proof to him.

Sasha also gave the name and address of a cousin
of his who had been a professor in the USSR and who was
now living with his mother in Cincinnati. He knew
several other Americans, too, and he gave me their
addresses.

On the final day of the book fair we were to meet
again. My schedule was very restricted, however, and
Sasha didn't show up on time at the rendezvous point.
I wondered if something terrible had happened to him.

When I arrived back in the United States, filled
with horror and revulsion at the terror I had seen and
heard about, I was anxious to write about my experiences.
I did write, but I wrote with a hand behind the back.[1]

There were so many stories I wanted to tell but couldn't; these were the best ones. For example, I had seen with my own eyes the harrassment Soviet police inflicted on honest people we had met, youngsters whose only motivation was to obtain information, but the stories would have to remain untold until the victims left Russia. I also was shocked at the behavior of the American officials in Moscow, diplomats so afraid of bad relations with the Russians that they wouldn't xerox a paper I had given over the Voice of America.

Definitely on the list of topics not to write about was the story of my three visits in a Russian Jewish home.

To compensate for the absence of articles, however, I had a new activity. My life was now filled with an unanticipated second phase of the trip. I was on a mission to dozens of people. Everyone I had met in Moscow had an assignment for me, a gift to deliver or a call to make. Among the first of the missions I undertook was my investigation of the life and death of Sasha's grandfather, Abraham Kurts.

I called YIVO, the Yiddish Research Institute in New York and reached the archivist. He invited me to YIVO headquarters on 86th Street in Manhattan. When I arrived, he said that he remembered that a letter had been written to the Polish government-in-exile in London by Emanuel Ringelblum of the Warsaw Ghetto. The letter, posted shortly before Ringelblum himself was murdered by the Germans, listed many of the prominent Jews, including actors, or so the archivist thought, who had been taken away by the German authorities.

Ten minutes of searching proved fruitful.

"Found it," he announced. We looked at the letter, a copy of which had been sent by the Polish government to YIVO years back, and there, in Polish characters, was Mr Kurts' name.

I immediately thanked the archivist profusely and ran to make some copies of the letter. But I knew that there would be a lot of trouble getting this list into Russia.

First, it was written in Polish. Second, it had been sent to the Polish government-in-exile in London. That was the wrong government-in-exile, from the Soviet point of view. They had sponsored their own such group; it was this government-in-exile in Moscow which had become the new government of Poland after the war. How would they allow something from the "bad guys" to pass their postal censors?

I had some extra time, so I went upstairs to the library where I spoke to the librarian, Dina Abramowicz, who had helped me to write my dissertation some years back; she had found important material for me then. As I told her what I needed, she said, "Maybe I can help you." She came back with a big, dust-covered book. Then my eyes recoiled in shock when I read the title of that volume: Lexicon.

"You are not going to believe this," I said to her. And the more I talked, the more I believed to myself that a miracle had taken place. I told her about the meeting in Moscow and what Sasha's mother had said. How, I wondered, had this woman in Russia, cut off from virtually every contact with the Western world, known about the existence of this book?

I asked Ms. Abramowicz to write an official letter stating that the library had information that Mr. Kurts had been killed in Poland, and I asked her to list where and when it had happened. I asked her also to put a big, official-looking stamp on the letter to impress the Soviet bureaucrats.

Then I called up Sasha's aunt, Retta, in Cincinnati. Together we formulated a letter to be sent officially to Sasha's grandmother, widow of the actor, from Retta. She would write that she had come across this entry by accident. She thought that "she would like to know about her late husband and about how evil the Nazis were to the great Soviet people and how they had tried to destroy Soviet culture."

We made many copies and sent them off at regular intervals, and as we subsequently discovered, at least one of them got through.

During the winter I was able to locate long-lost relatives of the Dranov's, a family in Albany, New York, that had settled there shortly after emigrating from Russia at the turn of the century. There were cousins living in Albany who were the same age as Sasha; descended from the same great-grandfather. Some of them had actually lived for a while with Sasha's paternal grandmother, a woman who had come to America and who had starred in the Yiddish theatre in New York for a time. Cut off from her son in Russia, she never knew what had become of him, nor he of her.

Sasha applied to leave Russia in late fall, shortly after my visit with him. During the winter, while we were all waiting for a response from the government, I

wrote but one letter to him. It was carefully phrased.
Key points mentioned were that he should not drag a lot
of furniture and books with him and that he would have
to wait several months, at least, in Rome before coming
to America.

At a little before eight o'clock one morning in
May, I received a call from Cincinnati. They had just
heard from Sasha. The government had given the whole
family permission to leave. They would be out in three
weeks or so. Then we heard that the time had been extended. Sasha was to call us upon his arrival in Vienna.

When the day came, there was no telephone call.
The next day there was no call. Nor was there a call
the day after that.

What could have happened? I spoke daily to Boris
and Retta in Cincinnati; we conjured up one atrocity
after another. Perhaps he had been dragged off at the
airport. Had he delayed because of illness? Maybe he
was shot for meeting with me.

Twenty days later, we finally received the call
we had been awaiting. Sasha had been robbed on his very
first afternoon in Vienna. He had lost our phone numbers
and had written to Moscow, to relatives, for them. Only
when the letter arrived from Russia could he contact us.

Sasha didn't know that in the free world you can
call "information." He also didn't know that you can
call "collect." And he also didn't realize that dozens
of people here in America were spending hours agonizing
over what had become of him.

My first request to Sasha was that he keep careful
notes of his experiences. I knew that personality
changes among people moving west from Russia were often
extensive and I had never seen them documented well.
A diary might be helpful.

Within two months my wife and I were in Italy. I
stayed for several days with Sasha and his family. Yuri
and Zoya and their daughter were also in Italy. Together we examined the transitory life of the Jewish
emigré in Italy.

We talked for a long time. Sasha reported that
he had been extremely depressed upon arriving in the
West. The days in Vienna, especially after the robbery,
were sheer misery. The Jewish emigration authorities
provided "guides" who were themselves recent emigrés
from Russia.

"They shout, pound the table, say 'you must do this
and you must do that' just like I was still in Russia.

The only difference here is that they call you 'mister,' not 'comrade.'"

Soon, however, he had become more active than he had ever been back in Russia. He got a job working for the Jewish immigration agency HIAS in Rome, translating from Russian to English. He moved his family into a small and shared apartment in Ostia, the port of Rome which now resembled a small Soviet city more than an Italian one.

What did he want to do? What would he do in America? Where would he live? What job would he get? How should he write his resume? What were the relative advantages and disadvantages of different parts of the country? Could he survive on his own or did he have to be near his relatives in Cincinnati or near me in Washington?

Meantime, Sasha organized English language classes on his balcony in Ostia. He raced home every day from Rome to teach his students. All the emigrés I met were taking English lessons. They were also preparing to enter a new world--physically, politically, emotionally, culturally.

One afternoon Sasha asked me to speak to the class. I talked about life in America. I answered questions that the students had. I recall my conclusion vividly.

"Many of you are asking about life in America, and you are asking me questions such as 'Will I get a job?' 'Where should I live?' 'Will I be able to afford a house?' and 'Will I be able to go to school in America?' You know, these questions can all be answered relatively easily and they will sort themselves out soon. You people were all strong enough to get out of Russia. That is not easy. You will all do well in America. But there is one thing that is more important than all the rest, I think, because it is so basic. Yet none of you have asked about it. It is the stumbling block for many of the Russians I know who now live in America.

"The Russians I know have the greatest trouble simply handling freedom in America. It seems to be too much for many of them.

"Every family I know, and I now know many, seems to fall apart in America. Husbands and wives start arguing, and divorce is an almost inevitable result. Suicide is not unheard of. My suggestion is to stop worrying about the details; these will work out all right. Start thinking about how to handle freedom in America.

"You will have to make a lot of choices. You have
no training in the making of wise choices. Make sure
that your decisions are responsible ones. Try to re-
strain your appetites and emotions and you will find
that things will work out well. Handle your freedom
wisely in America."

At nights we walked together through the streets
of Ostia. At the post office, hundreds of Russian Jews
congregated daily. There they exchanged information;
facts conveyed there carried far more weight than the
words of officials at HIAS offices in Rome. Some people
tried to sell items they had dragged from Russia. It
was evident that families were often quarreling. In
Sasha's own family, I felt that trouble was brewing.

One day I went for a long walk in the park with
the former executive, Yuri. Yuri had worked himself
up from the status of laborer to head of several bottling
plants in the Moscow area. He had given up a relatively
high status in Russia, exchanged it for the unknown in
America. He wanted to enter the business world. He
was exceptionally industrious. Every morning at seven,
Yuri arose to study English, and kept with it all day
long. In Moscow, he had known virtually no English;
in Ostia he was carrying on lengthy conversations with
me. It was remarkable.

I found that Sasha was somewhat disoriented by the
experience of leaving Russia. The effect of the new,
Italian environment on his personality appeared to be
extensive. His wife expressed deep anxiety about his
allocation of time and apparent lack of focus. He
showed up at home erratically, frequently lost his books,
or other valuable documents, and often had to be two
places at once. I worried that he would have trouble
settling down in America and I hoped that he would settle
near me, so that I could help guide him. Sasha was a
great intellectual, and whether his problem was over-
commitment or simply the anomie which often affects those
changing from one set of norms to another, I did not
know.

After my return to Washington, I received a call
from him early one September morning.

"Joe," he shouted into the phone, "my wife just
fainted."

"What's the matter?"

"We are being sent to Houston. We don't want to
go there. Would you please see what you can do?"

I raced around to the various Jewish authorities

responsible for these assignments. The experts all told
me that this was actually the best city possible.
Houston was rich and it contained a successful Jewish
community. The Soviet Jews in Houston were all doing
well, and the Jewish agencies would provide support for
the entire family. New York or Cincinnati couldn't provide as much, they said. Washington could not take any
more Soviet Jews. Baltimore would, but the Russian Jews
settling in Baltimore were not finding jobs.

"We recommend that you counsel your friend to take
the Houston offer. It's in his best interest."

After speaking to a variety of other "experts,"
all of whom agreed with the first that Houston was a
gold mine, I sat down and wrote a lengthy letter explaining the reasons for going to Houston. It would
be the best city in which to begin. Should they not
like Houston, they would have only to recall that the
United States is not the USSR and that they could leave
for any other city at any time.

Within a few weeks I heard from Sasha again. They
knew the very date on which they would arrive in America.
With my wife, I drove up from Washington and met the
family at the airport. Together with Sasha, his mother,
his wife, and his daughter, were Yuri and his wife and
daughter. All were bound for Houston. One night in
New York was too brief to be meaningful, I am afraid.
We did manage to visit the family with whom the Dranov's
had shared an apartment in Ostia. The man, a house
painter by profession, had begun to work almost immediately after arrival in America. The family rejoiced
in its Brooklyn location, in spite of the fact that the
husband asked me if I could help him obtain permanent
residence in a beautiful district named "Marlboro." He
had seen an ad about it, featuring a cowboy and a cigar-
ette, in an American magazine. As I watched his aged,
highly intelligent father playing with the dials on his
new color television set, I had no doubt that the truths
about relative economic strengths of the two countries,
as well as numerous other comparisons, were now sinking
in on these graduates of a lifetime of Soviet propaganda.

When the Dranov family landed in Houston, they were
greeted by a representative of the Jewish Family Service
association. They were taken immediately to a new apartment; Yuri and his family were given one close by. Sasha
found a temporary job within days. Klara enrolled in
a school for bookkeeping and the child entered public
school. Mrs. Kurts, hoping to resume her acting career

here in America, gave her premiere American performance
not much later, and Sasha joined her in a radio show
about the Yiddish theatre in Russia. Sasha soon jumped
to a better job and his mother was given an apartment
in a new building especially reserved for Jewish senior
citizens.

All was not to be rosy for Sasha and his family,
however. Within a few months of their arrival here,
serious cracks developed in the marriage. Klara moved
out. Roughly six months after their arrival here, Sasha
and Klara were divorced. Klara then married another
Russian immigrant and moved, with the child, to Oklahoma,
where her new husband had obtained an excellent position
with an oil company. Yuri did well by securing an excellent managerial position in Minnesota; and so before
the year was out, he had moved away.

For Sasha, matters deteriorated. First, his mother
was mugged. Then, following the troubles in his marriage, Sasha lost his job. Because he was newly arrived
and had not yet been granted a permanent residency here,
Sasha had had trouble getting the papers to Mexico, which
his job required. Major differences between the Soviet
and Houston cultures on office procedures, work habits,
and so forth, generated difficulties for Sasha. Then,
he landed a job as head of a language school. The owner,
however, was a charlatan who paid with rubber checks.
His English and translation abilities were sufficient
to generate a permanent contract with the U.S. government,
but the chances of being assigned as an interpreter grew
increasingly remote as the international atmosphere
clouded up in late 1979.

As I write, it is now slightly more than a year
and a quarter since Sasha set foot in the "golden land."
It is little more than two years since he applied to
leave Russia and little more than a year and a half since
he entered the free world. Has he changed?

More importantly, has he Americanized?

I have found that it is not easy to analyze this
question and the various answers it provokes. The basis
for the relationship we developed in Moscow was Sasha's
ability to speak fluent English. There were no barriers
to mutual exchanges of ideas and plans. At the same
time, one tends to find someone who speaks one's own
language more similar in matters of culture than he
really is; we can easily be deluded by language, and
if we are not careful, overlook amazing gaps in culture
and personality.

Since I have not kept a running diary, it is hard
to answer the above questions with assurance. Some
changes in the man are obvious, though. It is amazing
to me how ill informed Soviets are about basic facts
of world history; until this summer, for example, Sasha
had never even heard of the Entebbe Raid by Israel. He
knew absolutely nothing about Jewish history, even
Biblical history, knew little about American or even
Western history and politics, and was acquainted with
no philosophy, sociology, or economics other than
Marxist, with few exceptions. He is now fascinated by
such topics, as far as I can tell, but the gaps in his
knowledge remain wide. It is a great pleasure to see
a man suddenly discover his Jewish roots, but it is a
novelty to have to explain basic concepts of the religion
to a grown man.

Of more significance to social science are the intellectual changes. In the USSR, Sasha had been incul-
cated with a world view which is totally dominated by
a single ideological orientation. This is so strong
that it may well last, to a greater or lesser degree,
throughout his life. To him, there exists the "capitalist" world and the "communist" world. The prospect of
using other methods of analysis, of viewing reality or
defining societies on other bases, is nonexistent for
him. I think that the education system of the Soviet
Union must be viewed as an apparatus run by a cult rather
than by a secular society, and I doubt that the intellectual blindness induced by the system in Russia can
be fully overcome. Russian emigrés in this country may
switch their loyalties from that land to ours, but the
vision of the world dichotomized as the Marxist-
Leninists portrayed it will remain.

In Moscow, Sasha mentioned to me once that he didn't
know if he could bear to leave the city where he had
spent all his life. "The streets, the buildings, the
people, they are all part of me," he said. "How can
I leave all of this?" Other Russians to whom I have
spoken also have talked of the land with a mystical fer-
vor that, to me, seems out of place in the twentieth
century, particularly among intellectuals who supposedly
prize ideas above terrain. Yet today, after a few wist-
ful looks back, and in spite of his fervent defense of
the "great Russian culture," Sasha seems to be quite
far down the road to accommodation with American life.
Perhaps contentment will follow. Still, it is a question whether or not he fully appreciates the vast

differences between this civilization and the one he
left behind; and I do not think he yet grasps either
the breadth or the beauty of freedom. His writings show
sensitivity to the full nature of Soviet totalitarianism, although he has never articulated the evils of the
system to me, and I believe that it will be a number
of years before he is able to do so. The memory is still
too raw and the perspective too far off.

When Sasha first began working in Houston, he was
assigned to a visiting Soviet delegation. He invited
them to his house for tea after a meeting in downtown
Houston. I called up on the telephone and was horrified
to learn that they were at his home. He assured me that
they were perfectly trustworthy, "safe." Perhaps so.
Perhaps, too, such liaisons provide an easier transition, since it is clear that there is a type of serious
anomie, normlessness, which affects arriving Soviet Jews
and generates major difficulties for them. Certainly,
an arranged meeting with Sasha's biologically close relatives from Albany elicited little warmth or desire
for the development of family ties.

While Sasha speeks fluent English, he is far from
acculturated. There are many facets of American life
which will take years to absorb. His adventures with
such material aspects of this society as frozen orange
juice, fragile teapots, and Teflon pans have been comic.
More importantly, he clearly invests too much credibility in television commercials, in casual conversations,
and in schemes offering immediate relief from serious
problems. I have noted the same inability to distinguish
between serious propositions and those proffered for
the gullible on the part of many Soviet Jewish immigrants; tragic results have occasionally been the fruit
of this problem in discrimination.

One aspect of special concern to me was the encounter with our free press. The full meaning and nature
of our media has not yet made its mark on Sasha; his
experience in Russia as an editor apparently failed to
prepare him for an understanding of American journalism,
with its lack of centralized direction and the absence
of a consistent party line in reportage. Similarly,
the workings of the education system have baffled him.
The idea of applying independently to several law schools
was particularly confusing, since, as he said, in Russia
you don't have to choose. There is one test and if you
pass it, they assign you to the nearest school. I guess
the problem is that here in America we have no "they."

The realm of finance has been an especially difficult one for Sasha. The use of checks naturally vexes those who have always walked around with cash to pay for goods or services, although unlike most Soviet immigrants I know, Sasha has had relatively little difficulty with bouncing checks. Taxes, however, have proven a source of considerable anxiety; I had to prevail on him to opt for payment this year when he sought to postpone from April 15 to an unspecified future date his rendezvous with Uncle Sam. This was no small matter, since interpreters are paid in gross amounts, with no taxes withheld. Buying at auction, moving household goods, judicious purchase at sales and through the classified sections of newspapers, are skills he has been acquiring slowly.

There have been bright spots, though, on such matters. Sasha's first telephone call to me conveyed his astonishment at the rapidity with which the instrument was installed. "Joe, we just put in our phone. It took twenty minutes. In Moscow, it took three years!"

Not surprisingly, Sasha trusts information on personal questions which comes from Russian sources, especially from other Russian immigrants, more than that which comes from Americans. No doubt such is the case with most immigrants, but it is a surprise in this instance since Sasha speaks such fluent English. Thus, although told on several occasions that universities often award scholarships to intelligent and needy students, Sasha apparently placed little faith in that intelligence until he met a twenty-year-old undergraduate at M.I.T., newly arrived from Russia who already had a hefty scholarship there. In general, he takes as truth those facts which appear in print in the New York-based Russian language paper, or in Russian language books, more readily than those which come to him in an English medium.

It is my judgment that it is still difficult for Sasha to exercise self-direction. Increasingly, however, he is striving to do that. Moreover, he finds it difficult to plan for the distant future, depriving himself or his family of security now for security in the years ahead. Both traits are understandable, of course. Much of the former problem results from the simple necessity of having to have guides to pass successfully through a world that, as Dewey said, can be a "blooming, buzzing confusion" to foreigners; much also is based on the Soviet system's emphasis on the welfare of society rather

than the individual and its deprivation of what we consider the natural human right to self determination.
The latter problem is similarly dependent upon contrasting demands of the two societies and the perhaps unique
religious and psychological development of our American
civilization.

In this regard it should be noted that the American
people have always prized the practical over the theoret-
ical or the romantic. It is part of our national
culture and has been observed by scholars since the days
of Tocqueville. Sasha has not yet acquired this aspect
of our national character, I believe. He continues to
be oriented toward the aesthetic or romantic approach
to life. He often appears to move by feeling and drama
rather than by a Weberian rationality. Could one expect
a former Russian, and a writer, at that, to behave differently? No doubt, it is this ability to steer clear
of calculated rationality that enabled Sasha to lose
a country, a culture, a family, and a series of positions
within two years, and still remain emotionally sound;
for most Americans, according to the theorists of stress
among our physicians, such equanimity would hardly have
been possible. Whether this socio-psychological makeup
will survive three years of law school, which Sasha is
about to undertake, remains to be seen.

Sasha is ready to begin his life afresh in this
land. Many sociologists have written of the "cultural
baggage" immigrants invariably bring with them; few,
though, have focused on the special baggage carted by
those fortunate enough to win their exit from totalitarian states. Certainly, the dynamics of being "born
again" in a freer environment are complex. For the
emigré, a new career, a new family, and a new culture
are waiting; all the skills we might suppose are necessary for the conquest of these new challenges are
possessed by him--especially those dealing with language.
What the future holds for him is not at all clear, but
we can project a successful adjustment to America with
a reasonable degree of certainty.

NOTES

1. Cf. the author's article "At Moscow's Book Fair:
Visitors to the Jewish Booth," The Nation, January 1978,
also "The Moscow Book Fair," American Educator, December
1977.

6

From Moscow to Houston: An Uneasy Journey of the Spirit

Alexander Dranov

My seventy-year-old mother stood in front of the
crowd, clasping the microphone, singing a Yiddish song.
I could see she was nervous. The crowd was only half
Jewish, the others were "Americans," the tenants of the
big new apartment building for the elderly that B'nai
B'rith erected in southwest Houston. They were holding
a monthly party for those tenants whose birthdays were
in the month of October. Friends had come from outside,
who did not even know each other, or that many of the
tenants were Jewish. Of course, they did not know a
word of Yiddish. And there was my mother, singing all
those old Yiddish songs. She could not speak English,
so when she saw me come into the room, she asked me to
speak to the audience. When people come to America from
all over the world--from Italy or Greece or Germany--
she told me to say, you listen to their songs and enjoy
them, even though you may not understand the language.
You are still able to appreciate their art. So I hope
that even though you do not understand the words, you
still can enjoy the songs.

Yea! gasped the crowd, bursting into applause. I
thought of a comparable mixed audience in Russia. Could
something like this happen there? Perhaps it could,
though by accident; a party like this would never be
permitted officially.

As a matter of fact, my mother had told me of one
instance when her Yiddish company was given a derelict
"House of Culture" in which to perform and, because of
the lack of any advertisement in that remote Russian
town, the house was filled with Russian peasants who
happened to just walk in after a day's work. The per-
formers were horrified, it was senseless to perform in
Yiddish in front of those dark, uncultured, Russian

peasants, sitting with their overcoats on, cracking black
sunflower seeds and spitting the shells all over the
floor. But there was no way to back out. The actors
started with their songs and sketches and dances. The
spectators stopped cracking seeds. The murmur of their
voices died down, and when the performance was over,
my mother saw that not one of them had left. But that
was an exception. Here in Houston, Texas, she did not
know what to expect.

   Her singing was a great success. Jews and non-
Jews alike were congratulating her, thanking her,
expressing their admiration. "I did not understand a
word," one middle-aged lady, dressed in sparkling red
and overhung with jewelry, said. "But I enjoyed every
minute of it." I think she meant what she said. Suddenly there was an old lady at the piano and the whole
crowd was standing still, singing God Bless America in
chorus. That beat me. To sing a national anthem just
like that? By the expressions on their faces, I could
see they meant what they sang. Who in Russia would ever
think of singing the national anthem at a birthday party?
At any party? Except, perhaps, at a party party. Not
even there. Just like that, voluntarily: "Great Russia
has Rallied Together the Undestructible Union of Free
Republics . . . " Unthinkable! Unless, of course, it
was officially "organized." The whole thing was just
the other way around!

   So that was how Americans felt about their country?
They would not hold pompous speeches about how great
their country was or read aloud newspaper articles about
national achievements in agriculture. Instead, they
would scold the government at every step and grumble
about the prices and tell each other how incompetent
Jimmy Carter is and complain about inflation and interest
rates. But they would stand to sing God Bless America
without being told to. And they would sit for a good
hour listening to Yiddish songs, though not understanding
a word, not by accident or as the result of an oversight
by some official who forgot to tell them not to. In
fact, there were no officials to tell you what to sing
and what to listen to.

   Freedom! Was this what my friend Joe Drew from
New York meant by it when I met him in Moscow? Yes,
that was it. But how am I to handle it? In Russia,
I hated being told what to do and what not to do, but
have I not become accustomed to that in a way? There
was always somebody to tell you what to do in every

particular situation. And even when there was not, you already <u>knew</u> without being told, <u>from experience</u>. You <u>were</u> supposed to do <u>that</u> in this situation, and you were not supposed to do <u>this</u> in that situation. Suddenly there are no rules because there is no game. Or perhaps there is, and I do not understand the rules!

But the world is big and full of pitfalls; the country is new and strange and unknown. What am I to do? Please, tell me. I am groping.

Take time. Look around. See for yourself. And take time. Oh, yes. It does take time.

When I first met Joe Drew in Moscow, I did not know that. He pronounced the word "freedom" with such passion that you could not resist its magic. In Moscow we watched, together, a TV report on the inauguration of the Book Fair; the ceremony was held in the Kremlin, and there were the usual speeches and ovations. Joe was disgusted. "Why do all those intelligent-looking people have to stand up and applaud in unison to whatever garbage that fat idiot is saying?" he fumed. "When the Mayor of New York was campaigning for re-election last year, one guy came up to him and threw a big cake in his face!" Joe was very proud. I was very amused. Was that what he meant by freedom? It certainly had its attractive qualities. But was that all there was to it?

I remember the day we met very well. He was standing in the booth of the Association of American Publishers--a small but conspicuous space, crowded by excited visitors. I decided I wanted to talk to this guy. But I had just been warned by some plainclothes fellows that I would do better by not hanging around the official premises. That meant I had better not give them a chance to speak to me again. But the temptation was irresistible. The boy looked so familiar, so Jewish, so much my age. Yet, he was from "there," from another world, so distant, so forbidden, so unreal. But the books he was showing were real, and the crowd blocked the booth, reading avidly.

I talked to him. He was surprised I spoke English easily. I felt he was immediately on the alert. So was I. I could not see what was going on behind my back. I did not want to have to speak to those ubiquitous guys a second time. "Let's walk," he suggested. We started moving around the booth, talking but looking around all the time. "Let's go into the street," I suggested. "At least nobody will overhear the conversation."

In the street we plied each other with questions.
He asked me about Shcharously. I did not even know who
he was. Joe exploded. "They are going to kill the guy
just one mile from here and you don't even know? The
bastards! That's how they keep you informed!" Then
I had an idea. "Look, Joe," I said. "There is much
I don't know and there is, perhaps, something you don't
know. Why don't we meet at my apartment tonight and
talk about it all? I'll meet you in the subway at six
o'clock. When you see me, just follow me, at a distance.
Okay?"

We did as we planned. I met him in the subway and
he followed me into the train car, then out into the
street and into the bus. Then I got off and he walked
behind me, at a distance, following me into my apartment
complex. By then it was growing dark. I circled the
big apartment building in which I lived and entered the
door opposite mine. I went upstairs to the landing on
the third floor which permitted an excellent view of
the approaches. Joe was coming up to the entrance. There
was no one behind him. Two minutes later he joined me.
Without saying a word, we stood at the window waiting
until it was quite dark. The area, as far as I could
see, was deserted. A babushka shuffled by below, but
she did not look like a tail. Still, I followed her
with my eyes until she disappeared around the corner.
When I was sure no one was in sight, I led the way out
into the street again, to the entrance to my apartment.
Three minutes later it was over. We were safely at my
place.

As soon as we arrived, my wife turned on the TV
set and my mother covered the telephone with blankets.
My friends were already sitting around the table, waiting. I had told them to come.

The situation was definitely unusual, but easy.
My friends laughed at the story of our precautions. My
mother did not. We knew there was nothing to laugh
about. My family was preparing to apply for visas and
that was no time for hoodwinking the secret police, no
matter how cleverly.

When Joe heard that my mother was a Yiddish actress,
he wanted to interview her. He had his tape recorder
with him. My mother hesitated. Then she agreed, but
asked him not to make it public. She was afraid.

Yet, she told him the whole story. I listened,
fascinated. So did my friends. None of us had heard
the tragic story of the Russian Yiddish theater in full.

Most of us did not even know the key facts of the story.
And it was the first time any of us, including my mother,
was ever interviewed by a foreigner, let alone an
American journalist. We knew it was dangerous. Those
who were going to emigrate had to be "quieter than water,
lower than the grass," as the Russian saying goes, to
avoid any trouble.

Joe left after midnight. We had talked our hearts
out and become friends overnight. We had two more nights
like that, with all of my friends assembling at the
appointed time, in the now familiar manner. I was very
excited. I felt that if there were people like Joe in
America, I would not be without friends in that country.

That was one of my major concerns. In discussing
emigration, my friends and I saw only one problem: new
friends. No problem seemed as difficult as that one.
"Americans are not as good friends as Russians are,"
was the accepted view. "You must know, Sasha," my
friends told me, "that you will never have friends like
us in America. Human relations are different over there.
They don't value friendship like we do here."

That indeed, was frightening. In Russia, your
whole life depends on friends. There are no communities,
there are close circles of intimate friends--people you
can share your everyday joys or sorrows with. I remembered only too well how much I had missed my Moscow
friends during the two long years I worked in Burma.
Now it was not a matter of two years. I was leaving
my life-long friends forever. I knew I would not be
able to see them again.

But Joe changed the whole picture. When I told
him about my worries and how glad I was I had met an
American friend like him, he laughed. "There are many
people like me in America, I assure you," he said.

That seemed logical. Was it possible that I had
just met the one and only American who seemed an ideal
friend? There had to be others like him.

In October 1977, one month after Joe left Moscow,
we applied for visas. Joe seemed the last straw. The
last little push that I secretly needed.

For fear of harrassment, I had to quit my job. My
mother, however, continued to perform with her Yiddish
company until the last day of May 1978 when we were
granted permission to leave. We had waited for eight
months.

While the wait was a normal one, I was anxious to
leave. However, when the departure date was scheduled,

at last, it was an anxious waiting time. I was suddenly
dismayed and asked for a three-week extension. I did
not know that in America Joe was beside himself with
anxiety over the delay. He thought I had been killed
by the secret police, or at least thrown in jail. (There
was no communication between us in the last few weeks
before my departure.)

On June 14, 1978, an Aeroflot plane lifted my
family and me off the ground in Moscow and two hours
later (Just two hours later!) deposited us in an airport in Vienna. Two hours! We could not believe it.
We were in another world. We were free!

Many times have I had to say that word: free. And
every time with a different connotation.

No sooner did we enter the gates of the free world
than a smiling short man came forward to meet us. "Are
you going to Israel or elsewhere?" he asked. We were
prepared for the question. "Elsewhere," I answered.
"This way," said the man, and we followed him, fascinated. Was it that simple?

He led us into a spacious room and we waited for
our luggage. When it arrived, the man said: "Open your
suitcases, please. You will have to leave some of your
stuff here at the airport. You cannot take it into town
with you."

As we obeyed, he proceeded to remove some of the
things like cameras and bottles of champagne from our
suitcases. I was numb with astonishment. We had gone
through a similar operation at the customs in
Sheremyetevo, the Soviet airport, two hours before. I
could not believe my eyes. It was the same thing all
over again! Just like in the Soviet Union.

My shock was great. It helped me little to learn
later that the luggage search in Vienna was caused by
the need to cut down the trade in cameras and foodstuffs
that the refugees from the Soviet Union engaged in, in
order to raise some money in Vienna and Rome. Each of
us had only $90 on us--all that the Soviet government
allowed us to take out. But the man did not care.

After rummaging through our belongings, he smiled
pleasantly. "Your car is waiting outside," he said.

We got into the car that was parked near the exit
and a silent Austrian driver drove us towards Vienna.
The unpleasant experience at the airport was almost forgotten. We were in Vienna!

About an hour later the car stopped at a small
building in downtown Vienna. "Hotel," the driver said.

We pulled our suitcases from the trunk and walked
towards our first Western home and went in.

A young man, a woolen sweater wrapped around his
throat, sat behind a shabby counter, looking very
annoyed and tired-of-it-all. The paint on the counter
was peeling. "How many of you?" he said in Russian.
His voice was hoarse. The tone, the wording, were so
familiar, I could not believe it. It was as though we
were standing before some Soviet official, one of those
I had hoped I would never again see in my life.

"Four," I muttered in shock.

"One room, second floor," he said hoarsely. "And
get your things out of the way."

It was so shocking I felt my blood boil. I contained myself and looked up the long staircase leading
to the second floor. What I saw surprised me even more.

At the top of the stairs stood an unmistakably
Russian woman, middle aged, overweight, a dirty apron
covering a huge belly, a frying pan in one hand. Her
attitude, the way she looked, her posture were so
familiar, I felt I was back in Russia, somewhere in an
Odessa backyard. The woman did not say a word, just
looked at the new arrivals. This was, then, what the
new life looked like.

I noticed a sign on the cracked wall scribbled on
a scrap of paper torn out of a school exercise book.
It read:

Putting food in the refrigerator without permission is prohibited. If found, such food
will be thrown away.
                    Administration

That did it. A typically Soviet warning on the
wall of a hotel in Vienna? My mind was turning. Who
wrote it? Who was the mysterious "Administration?" Were
they Austrians? Soviet? Was there no getting away from
the Soviet way of life? Will it continue to pursue me
around the world?

I could not imagine then how long it would take
me to get away from it.

The four of us were put in one room with two beds
in it. We knew that emigration was not exactly going
to be a path of roses, but this was far below what I
had expected. But then, we were lucky: the next room
contained three different families, men and women together.

The "Administration" turned out to be the same
annoyed-looking former Soviet who had met us in the
lobby. There was not a single Western official to speak
to. And the young Russian was administering the place
in familiar Soviet style. "You do not like it? Well,
nobody invited you here."

That was the attitude I was to encounter, later,
at every stage of the long emigration ordeal. "Nobody
invited you here. So do not complain." "You have not
received your quota of daily expenses from HIAS? Never
mind, you will have to pay it back anyway. So the less
you get, the less you pay." That was what many of us
were told. We thought that was the HIAS policy.

Such was the shocking pattern both in Vienna, and
later in Rome. The next morning after we moved into
the hotel in Vienna, we went to register with the HIAS
office. The day was lovely. A colorful streetcar took
us past the Vienna opera along the well-trimmed boule-
vards. A pleasant sound of the bell announced each stop.
We were in Vienna! Underground passages were not drab
like in Moscow, but full of light, luxurious shop-
windows and sidewalk cafes.

But the HIAS office was full of irritated, tired,
exhausted emigrants. They were sitting on benches along
the walls. A guard at the door snapped at those who
asked questions. HIAS officials were evidently hidden
somewhere behind closed doors.

But after all, it was right in a way. What did
I expect? A carpet and a motorcade? Nobody invited
us here. It was true.

We waited interminably. There were piles of forms
to fill out and I spent the waiting time doing that.
That was familiar, too.

A few hours later I discovered that my wallet had
been stolen. It contained all the dollars I had gotten
from the Soviet government and the receipts for my
baggage. "Don't worry," I was told. "It often happens
both in Vienna and in Rome."

On the way back to the hotel in the evening, Vienna
was shining at us. But we seemed separated from it by
a sort of invisible wall. We could see it all, we could
see the West, the free world. It was there, but we were
not part of it. We were emigrants, strangers, aliens.
We did not belong there.

A week later we were in Italy. Rome! A dream come
true.

But here again, it was not like what I expected. The

untidiness and garbage in the streets around our hotel was appalling. The water in our hotel room did not run. There was a deafening noise from the street. Even at night. The walls of buildings were covered with slogans painted in charcoal. Even the subway was littered with garbage. The insides of traincars were mottled and dirty. Very often I would see a hammer and sickle painted in thick red on the walls.

Still, it was Rome; and I tried to forget the unpleasant side. But it was not easy.

In the HIAS office on Via Regina Margherita, we were handled in the same familiar Soviet-type fashion. And no wonder: the first HIAS officials we came in contact with on entering the HIAS office were Soviet emigrants like us--young boys and girls hired by HIAS to help process the multitudes of new arrivals. These boys and girls instructed us on how to fill out forms and answered our numerous questions. And their welcome was far from cordial. Untrained in the art of social work, steeped in the same old Soviet-type attitudes, very often rude, impolite, and impatient, those emigrants-suddenly-turned-into-officials gave us the same type of treatment from which we had fled: they pounded the table, dismissed complaints, ignored questions, and so on. True, they addressed us as "misters" rather than "comrades." But that was the only difference from the old times.

To make fun of the situation I started addressing my fellow emigrants as Tovarishi gospoda, "comrade misters," which sounded very ironic in Russian. But it was wry humor.

American workers of HIAS, apparently, were too busy to supervise the behavior of these young people, or maybe they did not care. That was what many of us felt. The treatment received resulted in a widespread feeling of frustration, even shock, among the arrivals. Again, I felt that we were neglected and isolated from the real West. I knew it could not be all that bad; but that was what it looked like to many of us.

Materially, true enough, we were well taken care of. All of us got special allowances to pay for the rent and food. To find a place to live, however, was entirely our own problem.

Emigrants seeking apartments gathered at the famous post office in Ostia, near Rome, which was a potboiler of rumors and information, as well as an apartment exchange. Here again, the emigrants ran the show. Convinced that here, in the West, one had to push everybody

else around in order to survive, some recent arrivals
were trying to make money at the expense of their fellow
emigrants. Some of them were very good at that. It
was already an established rule, when we came to Rome,
that the emigrant who vacated an apartment the day he
was ready to board a plane to America charged a special
price for letting another emigrant take the vacancy.
The price often exceeded the monthly rent charged by
Italian homeowners. Apartments were hard to find, so
there was no way out. You had to accept the terms and
do the same thing to the next lodger in order to re-
cover your money. It was a vicious circle. Some clever,
unscrupulous fellow must have started this chain reaction
long ago.

I was hired by the HIAS office in Rome as an interpreter. My duties were to help one of the American case-
workers interview new arrivals. I hated to be part of
the "Soviet team," but I needed to earn some money after
I had been robbed in Vienna.

A few days after I started work I received a tele-
gram from Joe. It came to the HIAS office. It read:

"WELCOME TO THE FAMILY OF FREE AND CIVILIZED MAN-
KIND!"

My dear friend Joe! He was one and only. I did
not feel particularly welcomed by the free and civilized
mankind. Even though I was working in HIAS, I still
did not feel I was part of that world.

During the two months that I worked in HIAS I saw
a great many of my fellow refugees coming from various
parts of the Soviet Union. They were a diverse lot.
But they shared some features in common: inflated expectations, false pride, distrust of officials, suspicion
of questions, anticipation of deceit. Very often they
twisted the truth, lying whenever it seemed to be of
benefit. Sometimes these people lied when there was
no benefit at all to be gained, just out of habit. Any
HIAS official, especially the friendly one, was sus-
pected of some hidden plan at the back of his or her
mind. A plan to take something away from you, to deprive
you of something that the others had: that was an idea
very firmly implanted in the minds of many. It was a
familiar Soviet concept that everybody must have as much
as everybody else. Or more. But not less.

In August, Joe arrived in Rome to see me. That was
just another incredible display of his friendship.

By that time, he had moved from New York to Washington, D.C., to teach at a university there. It was also time for me to decide where I wanted to live and work in America.

There was a question on the HIAS form: where would you like to live in the United States? But the choice was not unlimited. It was limited to cities in which Jewish communities could support a family for the first few months until someone in the family found a job. More and more cities were announced "closed by the HIAS."

I wanted to go to one of the cities I knew something about: Boston, New York, San Francisco, Los Angeles, Washington, D.C. But I was told that out of these five, only New York was still open. The others were "closed." Instead, my caseworker offered me another one: Houston.

Houston? No! I did not want to go to Houston. My family wanted to go to a big cosmopolitan city with a lifestyle like in Moscow. But HIAS officials insisted on Houston.

It was a big city, they told me. A growing city. A booming city. A comfortable city. A good job market. Heat and humidity? That was taken care of by air conditioners in every apartment, in every office, in every car. And later after I had gotten settled and could be on my own, I could move wherever I liked.

New York, on the other hand, was bad, I was told. Everybody was leaving New York. It was a dying city. It was filthy. It had no jobs. And it was not American. It was a jumble of national communities cooped up within themselves. It was not the right place to integrate into American society.

Houston was.

I spoke to Joe. I told him I wanted to go to Washington, D.C., where he lived. He said he would find out and write to me after he got home.

As always, Joe kept his word. His letter came a month later. My family and neighbors assembled in our Ostia apartment to hear me read it out loud.

"After inquiring at every appropriate office in Washington and New York," Joe wrote, "and after consulting with many people who are in a position to know, Houston seems to be your best choice. Everyone I spoke to is confident that you should go to Houston. I feel I must support this idea even though I would love to have you here in Washington." Reasons? Same as given by HIAS.

Joe's authority was beyond doubt.

On September 20 a huge 747 landed me and my family
in New York. We were in America! And who was the first
to meet us at the airport? Of course, Joe. He had
driven from Washington to meet us.

The next day we got off the plane in Houston, Texas.
We had reached our new home.

The difference with Moscow, Rome, and New York was
enormous. The city looked like a huge parking lot.
Everyone drove a big crocodile of a car. At rush hours
the freeways were jammed: there was no subway and everyone drove in a separate car. The waste seemed absurd.
So much gas and power to drive one person to or from
work? The person per car ratio in Houston is said to
be one to one. Sometimes it seems even less than that.

But was not comfort one of those things that had
attracted me in Russia? Oh yes, to be sure. But in
Houston it was not long before I discovered the other
side of it. People were separated from one another.
By their cars, houses, and comfortable offices. Even
on weekends I could see lonely figures in the driver
seats. For me, there was not much comfort in comfort.

Separate one- or two-story houses. Beautiful. Rows
of one- or two-story apartment complexes. Ugly! But
comfortable. Privacy, at last. But isolation, also.
Comfort and isolation.

One of the things I still cannot get accustomed
to is that there are no sidewalks for pedestrians in
Houston. So people do not walk, they drive. They drive
even to the nearest mailbox. Or a store. Or a bank.
Drive-in bank, drive-in food, drive-in theater. People
never walk. At best, they jog.

So there is not much chance to see or meet people
informally. The only place you can see them is a
shopping center. Or a community center.

The Jewish Community Center was the first place
my family and I visited when we arrived. It was a magnificent building. A Jewish Center! Something unthinkable in Russia.

And, of course, it seemed the right place to begin
my acculturation. It was the place for the Jewish community to get together. It was the right place to meet
friends and find something to apply myself to.

Center membership for the first year was free for
the Russian emigrants. It was very thoughtful of the
community leaders.

Yet, I found it hard to integrate into the life
of the community. The functions, brunches, and seminars

that I attended were sometimes interesting to watch, but I remained a spectator. I tried to participate in some of them. But I found it hard to meet people who would share my interests or desires. People were friendly, polite, but detached. "Plastic" was the word I learned later.

My mother, a Yiddish actress, was with me. She offered to perform. She thought that a Jewish Community Center was the right place for a performance in Yiddish. But the Center leaders were not interested.

Still she gave her first performance for the Center Senior Adults in January 1979. There were about 200 people. The reception was very enthusiastic. I thought she had managed to break the ice.

Yet, the Center leaders showed no interest in having my mother perform again. I could not understand it. She had several good shows to offer. They were in Yiddish. They had to do with Jewish life. I would give the gist in English so that everybody could follow the story. The audience had loved her first performance. The reviews were excellent. Yet, there was no enthusiasm on the part of the Center leaders. The Performing Arts Department was busy putting on a stage version of Ten Little Indians in English. The subject did not seem to be Jewish at all. But the department was much more concerned about it, we were told the schedule was "full" throughout 1979.

I joined the young Center members who wanted to act in Ten Little Indians. There was an audition. I auditioned but was rejected. Well, maybe I was not good enough. But what the Center leaders failed to see was that my mother and I were trying to get involved in the community. They did not seem to appreciate that it was more than just another Center activity. It was a way to help us Russians to acculturate and participate in the community life in the way that best met our interests. There was no other place we could go. I was beginning to see that joining the community was not going to be easy.

My mother did give a few performances in synagogues and private homes. But each time I had to work hard among the Houston Jewish community promoting her show. Community leaders were not interested even though the show was free and the audiences were more than enthusiastic.

The situation with other Russian refugees was worse. They, too, tried to join the community. But on top of

all other problems, they had a language barrier to overcome. So for them it was even harder. Soon there was
a common feeling among the Russian immigrants that we
could not find a common ground with our Jewish bretheren
in Houston. We were too far apart. Some began to
feel even more pessimistic: we will never become
Americans. Perhaps our children will.

We went to synagogues. There were seven of them
in Houston. Magnificent buildings. There was an opportunity to be a Jew, an opportunity all of us were denied
in Russia. So we started going to Sabbath services every
Friday. It was something new and unusual. But the
meaning of what was going on did not reach most of us.
None of the Russians knew anything about Jewish religion
or Jewish history. And there was no one there to explain
or educate us. So we just sat as spectators in a theater
watching a play in a foreign language we could not follow. Again, we felt separated from the others. We were
Jews, but we were different.

Occasionally there would be an attempt to help us
acculturate. Every year in October, the Beth Israel
Synagogue holds special Friday service for the Russian
refugees. The new arrivals are asked to come forward
to hold the unfolded Torah while Rabbi quickly reads
excerpts from it. The Rabbi is usually the one who
enjoys it the most. The Russians just stand there trying
to follow the story and feeling awkward on display in
front of the full house, as in a showcase. And then
the Rabbi finishes the story and it is all over. Exit
the Russians, as distant as before. A good symbolic
affair, perhaps. A kind of consecration. But not more.
It is left at that and later dismissed by the Russians
as meaningless. A kind of pokazukha [something done
for show], American style.

This year, the Jewish Community Center tried something different. It arranged a Seder for 200 Russians,
with the Rabbi presiding over the ceremony and saying
prayers and explaining their meaning through an interpreter. That was a good evening. The next week the
Jewish weekly published a report on the function, com-
mending the Rabbi and the Jewish Family Service for
bringing the Russians in on a Seder. But no Russian
was ever asked how he felt about the whole thing. Nobody
really cared about how we felt. To Russians, again,
that evening was a one-way street. There was no inter-
change between us and them. In fact, to many of us, it
was just an occasion to be together among ourselves--

a long-felt necessity.

This situation has led to the locking of the Russians within their own little community. Occasionally somebody is invited by a well-meaning American family to a Sabbath dinner or something of that sort, but that is rare and no personal relationship is usually formed at such gatherings. Names of invitees are often picked from a list at random and when the hosts meet with the guests, there is little ground for anything more than polite cordiality.

There are very few Russians I know who have found close American friends in Houston. In fact, few even visit with anybody outside the Russian community. I, myself, know only two or three American homes that I can visit and then only once every two or three months. A far cry from my friendships in Moscow, or from my expectations.

It looks as though my friends had been right in warning me. Typical as Joe said he was, I had not found anybody like him in Houston, Texas.

But even with him there were problems. In June 1979 less than a year after I came to America, my wife left me and moved to another state with my young daughter. There she married another man, a Russian emigrant. My shock was great. Two months later I lost my job. Another month later, my mother got mugged in the street. The world seemed to be falling apart. Unable to stay in Houston any more, I went to Washington, D.C., to stay with Joe for awhile. He was my only friend, after all. That meant that I had somebody to go to in time of crisis.

When I came to see him I felt very depressed. So depressed, in fact, that he thought I needed a counselor. But he could not, he said, see the reason for my depression and apathy. Of course, a divorce was an unpleasant thing, but how could I be so unable to control myself? Three months had already passed after it! In Joe's estimation I should have gotten over it in three weeks.

Now, he was in a position to know. He was a sociologist after all. And an American. Oh, yes, he was an American.

"I cannot understand you Russians," he said. "I have known many of you. And the pattern seems to be the same. You are too emotional. Too irrational. What's more, you tend to inflate your emotions. You are unable to control them."

Yes, that was true. Emotional ties of any kind seem

to be much stronger with us Russians. It seems to be
harder for us to leave places and people we love behind.
In Russia I was giving lectures to English teachers about
American cultural patterns. "America," I said, "is a
nation on the move. An average American moves every
five years." Yes, I knew that. Still, it is hard for
me to understand an American who leaves his hometown
for another because of a job offer paying two or three
thousand dollars more. Everything else is usually
secondary.

A young man I know in Houston, a recent arrival
from Leningrad, refused an offer of a job paying $20,000
a year because it involved relocation from Houston to
Omaha, Nebraska. He felt he did not want to move there.
He had gotten used to Houston in the five or six months
he had lived here. He did not have any other offer
for a long time, and his wife's salary as a laboratory
technician was barely enough to make ends meet in the
family. Finally, he accepted a position in Houston
paying less than $15,000 and on a much lower level than
in Omaha. Another reason for that was that he did not
want his wife to quit her newly found job in Houston.
And he could not think of going to Omaha alone and
leaving his wife behind for a couple of months.

Family ties seem to matter much more to Russians.
Traditionally, Russian children and parents stick together much longer and more closely than Americans. I
know many Russian Jews who cannot leave Russia because
their elderly parents won't go. We are much more supportive of each other than Americans are even though
we do not like to live with our parents any more than
Americans do.

On the other hand, Russian marriages break up easily
in America. It is usually the woman who does it. Whatever family tensions had existed in Russia could not
easily be resolved by moving out. There was nowhere
to move. The wife had to endure no matter what. In
America, she suddenly feels independent. She can earn
her own living, move or leave. And she does it, taking
advantage of the new freedom. So, to Russian men,
American freedom has its other side.

Russian women have been noticed to find American
husbands much easier than Russian men find American
wives. One of the reasons may simply be the woman's
better adaptability to partners, or so some of the
Russian women I know claim.

Whatever the reasons, emotional adaptation to the

new life is very difficult for many of the Russian emigrants, even when they are financially and professionally
well settled. Surprisingly, these emotional problems
do not always decrease with years. Added with time is
often nostalgia.

Adaptation to American cultural patterns is not
easy either. The radio was one of the first things that
surprised me. Instead of endless propaganda stories
that could drive you crazy in Russia, here, in America,
one can hear music in his car from morning until night.
An unusual joy. But soon I discovered that most of the
Houston radio stations broadcast the same type of country
and disco music every day. I have not yet developed
a taste for it. There is very little foreign music on
the radio in Houston. In Russia, we did not have much
music on the air but what we had was more diverse, if
you knew the right time to tune in.

On television, the colors and camera work are fantastic. New programs are unquestionably superior to
Soviet propaganda. Children's programs and cartoons
are very good. But there is little to see in the way
of films and shows. Films are often little more than
primitive gun shooting and murder stories. Killings
and horseback riding dominate the shows. There is little
to think about, hardly any opportunity to indulge your
aesthetic sense. Good shows are numbered. Of those
that I like, I can name only one or two, like "Laverne
and Shirley" or "Benny Hill." Occasionally, Johnny
Carson. Yet some of his allusions are still wasted on
me, let alone those Russians who have not yet mastered
the language.

And then there are commercials, those pillars of
American life. I get so annoyed by them that often I
choose not to watch TV at all. Joe told me he was able
to disengage from the commercial completely when he
watched a program he liked. I cannot. It is another
skill I have to acquire. Commercials are done so well
most of the time that I cannot disengage, though I hate
to watch the same stupid thing for the fifth time. As
a result, I cannot enjoy a good film or show because
my emotional and mental involvement is destroyed and
the artistic impression is ruined by incongruous inter-
jections.

I discussed American television with some of the
educated Americans I know in Houston. I told them that
no Russian would like to see primitive shooting and
killing stuff on television in such quantities. I did not

think such films could have a regular audience in Russia.
If that is what the American public likes, the average
Russian, then, is more sophisticated than the average
American. In fact, that observation was confirmed by
other things, too.

How could it be that an average American or, let's
say, Houstonian, comes across as a less-cultured or
sophisticated person?

One of the reasons seems to be the general standard
of secondary education. In Russia it is free and com-
pulsory and its standards, which are rather high, are
universal. College education in Russia seems less
specialized and more general than in America, with a
lot of time wasted on the study of useless ideological
disciplines. But secondary and high school education
seems to be more efficient and diverse.

Added to that is the fact that everyday problems
of life have apparently made the Russian more sophisticated and adaptable to stressful situations. The difficulty of going through everyday life has made the Russian
capable of doing many things himself and of considering
a great number of factors in making quick decisions.
This is apparently a school of everyday life that few
Americans have ever been through. The entire Soviet
way of life is such that you simply have to know or
understand many things, including human psychology,
social organization, ways to get things done, that an
American need not know about to be equally or even more
comfortable or successful. That "extracurricular" education in Russia is universal. This is even more true
of those who have gone through the emigration trial.
So many Americans do seem simple to us.

Culturally, too, Russians seem to be better equipped
than Americans as a general rule. In part, this is due
to higher standards of high school education and a more
general college education, which gains in
breadth at the expense of depth. The other side of this
difference is much higher specialization and profes-
sionalism in American society, which is precisely the
factor which makes it more efficient than the Soviet
system. It is surprising, isn't it, that while a social
system is gaining in efficiency, people would be losing
in versatility.

Russians read more. It has become a truism, but
it is true. The explanation is simple. Given the limited
choice of leisure time possibilities, the Russians have
developed a habit of reading. Plus the fact that the way

of life itself is very conducive to reading. A developed system of public transportation is a major factor in making reading a national hobby in Russia. Americans are unable to read as much, or at least as often, even if they wanted to. You cannot read books when driving a car. But you can read several pages, often as much as a chapter or two, in a subway or on a streetcar when going to and from the office. Russians love to read, particularly anything translated from foreign languages.

Another factor that seems to contribute to the cultural difference between us and Americans is the role of the media. The Russians reap the benefits as well as the disadvantages of the controlled exposure to the arts on television, radio, and the press. Because the box-office response is not a factor, Soviet arts tend to be more educational and less dependent on public taste. The quality of films, including Soviet-made movies, has been, until very recently, often superior in psychological content or artistic value to the flood of crime or gun-shooting stuff on American television or in the cinema. Crippling as the controlled art or media can be, it can try to avoid showing things that caters to bad taste. It a is declared principle of Soviet cultural education through the media to raise standards of public taste rather than go down to meet them. The effects of this policy are felt throughout the nation. The Soviets certainly lose in standards and quantity of information, but seem, at least somewhat, to gain in standards of cultural taste.

In America, my Houston friends told me, that was out of the question. Who is there to decide what is good or bad for the public? The public itself dictates what it wants to see or hear. That, in my view, is exactly what leads to the relatively low standards of popular taste in America. But what can be done about it? The general critical attitude to the role of the government in this country rules out any possibility of government control of the arts.

But I still wonder whether there can be a way of controlling the quality and standards of television production (One could do without the Gong Show, don't you think?) and media content in general, without sacrificing the ideals of the free press. Is it that difficult to provide better artistic values without impairing the freedom of information? There are necessary limits to freedom, anyway.

There is another factor which stands out when you

compare American and Soviet cultural patterns. Isolated
as it is from Western culture, Russia has always tried
to get to know as much about that culture as it could.
America, having no problem in communicating with Europe
(other than geographical, perhaps) has remained largely
self-interested. Few Americans care or know about
foreign countries unless their interests are affected
in a particular way. Today there is more awareness of
what is going on in Iran and the Persian Gulf because
America's immediate interests are at stake. There is
some interest in Japan because that is where the gas-
saving cars are coming from. But other than that--
little. The average American seems to know much less
about other countries, including Russia, than a Russian
knows about other countries, including America. That,
despite the fact that the information system in Russia
is by far inferior. But here again, the share of the
news about the world is much greater in Russia than in
America and the popular interest in the way other
nations live is much more persistent among Russians.

That may be partly due to the common feeling the
Russians have that no matter how much they know about
their own country they are unable to change anything.
In America, people feel that they ought to know what
is going on in their own country in the first place,
in order to be able to influence the course of events
through the use of democratic tools available to them.
Another explanation, perhaps, is that Americans have
always been convinced that their country is by far the
best and richest and most plentiful, so that there has
not been too much interest in foreign things. Now that
this feeling is no longer so strong, this attitude seems
to be changing.

Another problem immigrants like myself are faced
with is the freedom of choice. In a number of ways,
life in Russia is simpler because often there is little
or no choice, whether it is something you want to buy
or see or live in or learn. In America, the immensity
of choice has puzzled, I am sure, every Russian immigrant.
Whatever we want to buy or see or hear or vote for, there
is a choice that we are unaccustomed to make. Often,
we are as frustrated by the choice here as we used to
be by the lack of it in Russia. If we do make it, we
have to get all the available information and to employ
all of our capacity for decision making. Decision making
is a baffling process, for we have to consider the staggering array of information on the entire spectrum of

factors involved: the price, the benefits, the distance,
the place, the climate, the family, etc., and compare
it to all the other options. And usually there is no
one to guide us through this maze of options to a correct, let alone simple, solution.

The flood of information in the form of books, reports, newspapers, magazines, special brochures, and
all forms of advertising is staggering. Consumer information is an institution we are completely unfamiliar
with. We try to cope by reducing the volume of information through the process of elimination for fear of
getting drowned. And it takes time to learn the simple
ways. In many cases, years. In some, I fear, a lifetime.

The use of information is a skill that I have not
developed. We come to America unprepared to use the
fantastic array of information sources. The use of telephones, directories, television, newspapers, brochures,
and ads, to get information we need is new to most of
us. The Yellow Pages is something we have never known
existed. In Moscow, let alone other places, I could
not get a phone directory. The only source of phone
numbers was a special telephone information service known
as 09. In many cases, it was not efficient. The ease
of getting information in America does not come natural
to most of us. Our phone habits are different. I have
observed this difference more than once. For purposes
other than conversations with friends, the Russians use
the phone much more seldom. And when we do use it in
this country for other purposes, such as acquiring some
necessary information, we are usually much more tense
and insecure and unable to carry on a lengthy conversation even when language problems are not in the way.
(Usually they are; Russians find it excruciatingly difficult to understand Americans on the phone, when they
do not see them.) But generally, speaking to an unseen
person on the phone is a much more difficult task to
a Russian, unless the person on the other end is familiar. Such conversations are usually strained, exhaust-
ing, demanding, and even frightening. In other words,
it is another important skill we have to learn.

Compounding this difficulty is the use of various
phone gadgets that were never used in Russia, such as
hold-the-line devices, three-way conversations, and other
contraptions used by Americans on a daily basis. Putting
somebody on hold, for example, is so unusual for many
of us that we are often awkward or impatient or nervous

when we have to do it. Americans, on the other hand, do that with amazing ease. Another American skill that still fascinates me after almost two years in America is the way any American can conduct a telephone conversation and speak to two customers in front of him all at the same time without showing any sign of working under unusual stress. I have never seen an American raise his voice or shout in the receiver or tell you "Don't you see I am talking on the phone?" which is a typical Russian reaction. To talk to three people at once and be polite with everybody else at the same time is, to me, a fantastic skill, indeed.

So communication of all kinds is a problem contributing to the feeling of isolation. There are hundreds of things I still pick up daily in plowing my way through a grocery store, in the office, at interviews, and so forth. Making a resume, preparing for an interview, writing letters to companies, meeting people-- these are skills all of us have to spend a lot of time learning. And giving up old ways does not happen easily either.

One more fascinating quality which is so surprising and difficult to acquire in America is patience. There have been countless times when I compared American patience when standing in lines (Lines happen in American stores, too, you know.) to Russian impatience and bad temper in a similar situation. Sometimes it seems that Americans are never in a hurry. They are poised and calm and polite--the most surprising of all. A streetful of cars will stop to let in one car from a side street--something impossible by Soviet standards. The "Drive friendly" sign is just as unbelievable. Politeness seems to be ingrained in the American national character. To a Russian, used to people being rude and pushing and yelling at each other, this is amazing. At first we are fascinated by it. But then we often mistake politeness and smiling friendliness for some personal feeling. When the mistake is discovered, we feel deceived, and annoyed. We realize that there is nothing personal to it, that the friendly smile and the polite "Can I help you?" or "It was nice talking to you" is just a phrase, a cliche. Sometimes it can even hide hostility. And we, in turn, learn to wear smiles and say all those nice little phrases. To many, it is just an art, another skill.

One of the popular jokes among the Russians now is that to do well in English, all you have to learn is eight expressions which will enable you to carry on a successful conversation with any American. They are: "Take it easy," "Don't worry," "Enjoyed it," "Delicious" (to be used at table), "Fantastic!" (to be used in any situation), "Hi!" "Bye!" and "Okay!" There is sad truth in the joke. I have seen people getting along with this vocabulary and earning praise from Americans for their English ("Your English is fantastic!"). This joke also says something about what Russians think of the primitive level of communication among Americans. An extension of the same joke is that your real progress in English is marked by termination of praise from Americans. ("Oh, they no longer praise my English. Thank God! It means I am making real progress.")

These are just a few of the problems we face in acculturating to the new life. There are many others. They are constantly changing from year to year. In fact, those of us who have stayed in this country four or five years find it hard to communicate with new arrivals. Their problems seem trivial and forgotten.

A few months ago, my mother and I attended a seminar in a Houston synagogue about the Russian families in Houston. The seminar was held for the congregation by the Jewish Family Service which is in charge of the Russian resettlement program in Houston. People stayed after the service on Friday night to learn about us Russians from those who knew.

The leaders of the Jewish Family Service did know what they were talking about. The Russian resettlement program in Houston has been in operation for seven years and the Family Service has gained a lot of experience. The speakers talked about the special character of the "third" emigration wave from Russia, of its special psychology, mentality, education, and family relations. What they said was very true and revealing. So these leaders did understand us! I was gratified when Solomon Brownstein, head of the Jewish Family Service, admitted:

"We know that Soviet Jews now coming to the United States are very different from our grandparents who emigrated to America at the beginning of the century. Those Jews of the 'first wave' were mostly tailors and artisans from the Pale of Settlement, uneducated and unaccustomed to the Western way of life. They stood out conspicuously among Americans and it was extremely hard for them to adapt to the new life. Their Jewish education and tradition, on the other hand, were strong and alive. The present emigration wave has no Jewish education and tradition whatsoever but these people are highly skilled and educated professionals, often holding M.A.s and Ph.D.s. They are not unfamiliar with the Western life-style and way of living. Their ability to adapt to the new life is by far superior to that of their fore-fathers and they are not easily told from native Americans. But they are a product of sixty years of Soviet rule, and Jewish education and tradition are prac-tically zero. Therefore, we should not be surprised that when these people get off the plane in this country their first question is not 'Where can I have my son circumcised?' but rather 'What job can I have?' That, as well as an apartment to live in, is their major con-cern and this is exactly what we are trying to help these people with.

"Yet, in spite of the seven years experience in resettling and dealing with these people, and in spite of the success of the program, we have not even begun to understand how to bring these people into our Jewish community. We have found that not a single synagogue in town has even one member on its committees respon-sible for liaison with the Russian community. Occasional efforts to bring in the Russians to participate in our activities have been rare and inefficient."

Now that was the truth! I was glad to hear that some of the leaders were aware of our problems.

Then there were questions about us. People asked and asked. And we kept sitting there, in the back row of chairs, and though the speakers were aware that we were there, it did not occur to any one of them to refer some of those questions to us directly. Again, we were just sitting there, watching the play while it was us, the Russians, they were discussing. I felt we were, again, a subject for discussion rather than actual living beings. We were present, we listened, but it was as though they were discussing the situation of Jews in Russia, across the ocean. And we were there, behind them, all the time.

Given the difficulties of our integration into the Jewish community, what, then, can be said of our inte-gration into American society in general. Out there, the prospects are even dimmer, I fear. To Americans, we are just another kind of immigrant--along with Mexicans, Cubans, and Italians. And, in fact, we are, or so many of us feel. Very few Americans in Houston really understand or care about what it is like to leave a country like Russia and come to live in a country like

America. "You are from Russia?" goes the typical first
reaction from a Houstonian. "I'll be damned! Hey, Bob.
Hold the elevator, I am coming! Well, nice talking to
you, man. And welcome to America!"

7 | Conversations with Russian Emigrés in Cincinnati

Ellen Frankel Paul

Pyotr K. has made it in America; he owns a home
in a middle-class suburb of Cincinnati, holds a good job
as a clinical engineer, and has mastered the intricacies
of English. Despite his profession of having accomplished a rather easy transition to America, the old
life in Russia still plays heavily upon his conscience.
He is a man who resolutely refuses to forget.

The passions and controversies that drove him to
associate with dissidents: and to distribute samizdat
in Moscow are still a conspicuous part of this ersatz
American. After five years here, he remains active in
supporting victims of oppression in his homeland. And
he rails adamantly against the lure of material prosperity in America, for the good life must never dull
his commitment to combating Soviet injustice and the
denial of basic human rights.

In Russia, associating with dissident writers and
intellectuals was his lifeblood, "I couldn't live without doing it." Having been raised by a father who re-
membeed life before the Revolution, and held nothing
but contempt for the Soviet regime, left its mark upon
Pyotr. Or perhaps it was his own ebullient, inquisitive
character which refused to accept the lectures on the
history of Marxism, with teachers and pupils simply
"going through the motions," the teachers treading
gingerly over the ritualized material fearful of engen-
dering student questions that might inadvertently ensnare
them in an "anti-Soviet discussion." Whatever the reason,
Pyotr could not lead a full life in Russia without
engaging in heretical behavior, behavior that could endanger not only his relatively comfortable work as an
electrical engineer privy to contact with foreigners
and foreign magazines and literature, but his very life.

Didn't he live in constant dread? Wasn't the KGB an
omnipresent subject of foreboding? He admitted to "fear,"
but not of the all-consuming or enervating variety.

"If they searched my apartment, I would be arrested
for sure, but I only shared samizdat with trusted
friends. Look, if they arrested me, a little dissident,
then it would mean a new purge, and then no one would
be safe, anyway." Despite two contretemps with the KGB
in the early 1960s in which he was asked about several
friends and pressured to become an informer, he was not
deterred from his dissident activities. "I talked to
KGB nicely. I didn't say anything about my friends,
and nothing happened to them. I never informed on anyone, and I suffered no reprisals. At work, KGB came
to our Department Number One, but they trusted me because I had a security clearance. They never bothered
me." Like everything else in the Soviet Union, the KGB
was, he felt, an inefficient bureaucracy with one
section mercifully ignorant of what the other was doing.
Somehow, he would simply fall between the cracks.

Miraculously, he seemed to be doing just that, until
one frightening day shortly before he was to leave
Russia. Suddenly he was summoned to appear before his
army commander; being a reserve officer, he was certain
that he would be drafted. Instead, inexplicably, he received an award and was sent upon his way. The military
authorities, apparently, had no knowledge of his imminent
departure.

Security not only depended upon falling through
the crevices of Soviet engines of oppression, but also,
Pyotr felt, upon the ambivalent policy of the Soviet
leaders towards dissidents and Jews. "The Politburo
needs them to get trade with the West, to get wheat and
technology. People read ads and hear rumors that no
more visas will be given after the Olympics. But they
don't want refusniks during the Olympics. They're pres-
suring people to leave." Pyotr echoed a refrain that
we would hear repeated by virtually all the emigrés:
"Helsinki and SALT were the greatest mistakes. The
American government always agrees because there is a
free press. Russian government will do what they want,
regardless of any treaty."

Pyotr views Soviet emigration policy as a nefarious
plot hatched in the Khrushchev period in order to eli-
minate the Jews by depriving them of certain positions
and driving them from the country. "The Politburo members are all Russian nationalists, hate all other

nationalities; but the others have their republics, so
they go after the Jews. But as a Jew, even this is not
as bad as the period of the Doctor's Plot. That was
the worst time; we feared even to go to the market, that
we would be killed by regular people. We believed rumors
that there was a letter signed by Jews asking for death
for the doctors and exile of all Jews. They want to
crush Jews now, but in a different way."

It was from Pyotr that I first heard of the enormous
contempt felt by the intelligentsia for "black marketeers," a loathing that would be reiterated by many emigrés: "I went to Israel as a tourist, and now I'm certain I made right choice coming here. I knew Russians
who went to Israel. They would leade same lives as in
Russia. They left because of black market activities,
not political reasons. Nothing was holy from their
profits; they will sell their friends."

* * * * *

Nikolai M. exudes the counter-culture motif of the
late 1960s. Although fast approaching forty, he lives
alone in a student flat near the University of Cincinnati
while training for the rabbinate. Life in America for
this pioneer emigré (His family was the third to arrive
in 1973.) has not been uneventful. A divorce, several
career changes, necessitated by the unmarketability of
his training as a film critic, and a recent interest
in discovering the roots of his Jewish heritage, have
propelled this former dissident into a life very different from the one he had known in Russia. With his
Russian friends, such as the K.'s who shared his subter-
ranean life in Russia, his present lifestyle finds no
favor; he resents being judged, and made to feel like
a miscreant, an outcast.

As we headed towards my car after our lengthy interview, I asked him why there was so much factionalism
and enmity among the emigrés, particularly those who
had been life-long friends. How could one entrust one's
life to a friend in Moscow, and now in America have that
friendship terminated over petty disputes about divorce,
lifestyles, etc.? I found this explanation intriguing,
but other emigrés thought it only superficial. "In
Russia," Nikolai related, "all our energies were directed
into political discussions, talks about human rights,
and reading and copying samizdat. That was all important,
it was the tie between us. Personality, other interests,

didn't matter. But when we came to America, none of
that was important anymore. The common energy was gone--
it was irrelevant. So, now we noticed other things about
our friends' personalities that we had ignored, or not
even noticed. It is all very petty, small animosities.
It is sad."

From early childhood, Nikolai seemed politicized,
and this sets him apart from most of the other emigrés
who could not relate childhood experiences that had made
them question the Soviet system. For the others, doubt
and dissatisfaction would appear much later in adulthood, perhaps with Khrushchev's "Secret" Speech for the
middle-aged generation, or the death of Stalin for the
elderly when life somehow miraculously went on, despite
the death of the great leader, and Russia was not summar-
ily attacked by the West.

But for Nikolai, a sense of alienation, of being
different and superior arose early in life, at the tender
age of four. "My first day in school nobody played with
me. My mother explained, never be ashamed, be proud to
be a Jew, you belong to an ancient people with a rich
culture. Other people hate us through envy. Your life
will be more difficult because you are a Jew. So learn
more, work harder to achieve something." Indoctrination
began early for Nikolai in kindergarten when his teacher
asked a provocative question. With the children seated
in a circle about her, the teacher queried: "When would
you feel worse; if your father was killed in the army,
or if enemies killed Commander Stalin?" Perhaps the
date, 1945, accounts for the near unanimity among the
four-year-old respondents, for Nikolai was the sole dis-
senter, proclaiming that the death of his own father
would disturb him more than the demise of Stalin. He
was made to stand and was subjected to an interrogation.
"Your father's death would only be your personal problem," the teacher remonstrated. "But if Stalin were
killed, it would be a problem for millions of Soviet
children. Your attitude is selfish, stupid." Nikolai
kept his mouth shut throughout the verbal assault, but
he did not feel that he was wrong.

In subsequent years, he mechanically repeated the
lectures on the history of the Soviet Union. "I knew
it was all lies, double thinking, 1984. Even the most
devoted communists realized this; a lot of them were
cynical, hypocritical." Like all the other emigrés,
Nikolai joined the komsomol with the same "cynical attitude" of bored indifference. But in 1957-1958 it seemed

as though change were possible, and he undertook the sec-
retarial position in his unit under the then current
theory that if good people entered the party, things
could be changed. But nothing changed. After hearing
of Krushchev's "Secret" Speech, Nikolai's antipathy towards the "whole system" became more explicit. He
shocked his father, a party member by virtue of his
officer status during World War II, with the vehemence
of his denunciations.

Nikolai's dissident activities began early in 1959
with the collection of forbidden poetry in typewritten
form. From 1965 on, these activities became more important to him than his official, legitimate professional activities. He boasted of possessing one of the
best collections of unofficial literature in Russia.
Amazingly, Nikolai's only contact with the KGB occurred
when he applied for his visa. Despite running a cottage
industry typing pool to reproduce the Chronicle of Current Events, his activities escaped notice. Again, I
wondered about the element of fear. "I was always prepared for a search. I tried to be careful; even my
friends didn't know the addresses of my typists. Why
wasn't I afraid? Well, every person develops a thresh-
old. If you go below, you lose self-respect, if you
can't even do this much. I couldn't just live without
reading this information--Dr. Zhivago, August, 1914,
the Chronicle. I felt I must take the risk. If I had
my collection, people would trust me to exchange. I
wasn't brave enough to participate in demonstrations
on Red Square. I didn't want to sacrifice my life. So
I took risks that I could.

Nikolai clearly recalls the incident that prompted
his quest to leave the Soviet Union. It occurred in
1959 long before emigration was a possibility. He had
just seen the film "La Dolce Vita;" he knew that some-
day he must live in a country where he wouldn't have
to bribe people to see movies, and trust to mere happen-
stance that he would be fortunate enough to find the
right person to bribe. Artistic freedom was the motive
which inspired Nikolai's flight, yet his immediate decision to depart was prompted by a Soviet mother-in-law,
who, while opposed to the emigration of Nikolai's family
and unwilling to sign the requisite permission forms,
had discovered his secret samizdat activities and was
threatening Nikolai with a denunciation to the authorities. He had to leave. Fortunately, his visa was granted
without the signature of his recalcitrant mother-in-law.

* * * * *

To the emigrés, the soviet system looms monolothic.
Impenetrable, removed from everyday life, it is something alien and certainly beyond the grasp of individual
control or analysis. Why discuss politics in Russia,
the typical respondent would say, when nothing will
change. "The next Brezhnev will be exactly like this
one, but maybe worse." Will the "system" perpetuate
itself indefinitely? Do you foresee any prospects for
change? When pressed, a few people offered rather dismal replies.

"Communism in Russia is like fascism in Germany,"
remarked one effervescent woman in her sixties whose
memories of World War II still remain vivid and terri-
fying. "It could be changed by war. But I greatly fear
war, its devastation; I wouldn't wish this. But the
system couldn't be changed from the inside. You never
know who the informer is in any group, so there will
be no trust. There were strikes in the mines. They
tried but failed because they were all arrested. But
even there the discontent was only material, over wages
and provisions. Some say people attend churches as a
protest. People don't like komsomol. But the Communist
Party is a net; you can't escape detection."

Another emigré responded similarly: "Nothing will
change. Why discuss politics? The problem is the
structure. One man will not change the structure. So
why discuss successors to Brezhnev? It will never
change."

"Look, the next leader will be the same," replied
a computer programmer from Kiev. "The Soviet Union will
be very strong for the next fifty years. You would need
a revolution to change it. It won't be destroyed for
now: It is a bad system, but built very strong. There
is a lot of inertia in the system, for example, it is
very difficult to push the local party units from above."

A former factory administrator, a woman in her mid-
forties, found politics to be largely irrelevant to her
concerns as a Soviet intellectual: "Politics is not
the main question. Sure, if Andropov would be the leader
that would be terrible because he's KGB." Then, what
is the main question? Life questions. It is great to
be someplace. What the world is? We would discuss these
life questions. Also, what we heard on Voice of America
about American writers , or the Middle East, or China.

The Politburo is a group of ignorant, uneducated people who want only to get for themselves. Why talk about them?"

* * * * *

"Somehow you should have tested for character," remarked a sensitive, intelligent former professor of engineering, as we discussed the shortcomings of our research design on the Russian Jews. "What happens to the human character as it develops under a totalitarian system?" I asked him to speculate on his own question. "The Russian character is one of pervasive fear. This is the dominant characteristic of all Russians. And the reason why they left. But, of course, most aren't aware of this at all. I'll give you some examples. I went to a Unitarian discussion group in Cincinnati. I thought the people were lying. It was impossible that they would display their true thoughts to strangers. Inconceivable! The same thing happened at work. I had to attend a vocational workshop. I was afraid to speak, but finally had to say something. So I said something general and vacuous. But this year I did better."

"Another example. I forced myself to talk to you. I have tremendous fears. This country is so open to spies. Look what happened to the Bulgarian, Markhov, in London. Some of the emigrés might be spies, but I fear that I would be killed if I speculated openly about this.

An intense young woman who had only been in this country six months offered a more malign view of the Russian character, one in which the Russian people were less the victims of a totalitarian system and more the willing accomplices in their own destruction.

"I began to feel something was terribly wrong with Soviet life five years ago. It was a period of personal problems. I lost my husband. I traveled extensively in my work as a surveyor. Most people don't travel. I began to realize that life in general was hard, not only my personal life. You see, Russians are submissive people. Historically, they need to be ruled. They don't want to take control of their own lives. Drink vodka and be oblivious; that's what they want out of life. Their spirits are broken. But somehow I was different. Maybe it's because I am a Jew. My Jewishness set me apart from the Russian mold . . . . But I must warn you when you talk to other immigrants, they will

not think things out as deeply as I have, they're a
broken people and they won't tell you everything they're
thinking."

* * * * *

Is life improving for the average non-Jewish Soviet
citizen, and is he satisfied with the system?
"Everything is getting worse," was a typical response, this time recounted by a former vocational
teacher in her early thirties. "There is nothing to
buy in the stores, even if you have money. No food.
No goods. The newspapers say things are better, but
they're worse. And there is no more freedom . . . .
Who is satisfied with the system? Well, salespeople
are satisfied because they can steal. Also service
people, because they, too, can steal. Famous sportsmen,
artists because they are privileged; but some of them
want to leave. Of course, all the black marketeers."
Oddly absent from her inventory of the satisfied was
any mention of party members. What about these apparat-
chiki? "They're not satisfied; they don't believe. They
only entered the party to make life easier for themselves." What about intellectuals as distinguished from
workers; who is more satisfied with the system? "Most
educated people are not satisfied. They get paid less
than workers. And they can't steal anything!"
A more typical reply came from a young woman, a
computer programmer: "The workers aren't satisfied;
they complain about how bad life is, but just economics.
They make comparisons. Two years ago you could buy sau-
sage, and now you can't. You can't buy bras and buttons,
and you could ten years ago. That kind of talk. People
expect more than they did twenty years ago. They have
more money in their pockets, but there are fewer pro-
ducts to buy in comparison."

* * * * *

In retrospect, what would the emigrés find agreeable
about the Soviet system? Repeatedly, transportation,
medical care, and the free educational system were mentioned. But, Nikolai, one of our dissidents, offered
a characteristically sardonic response. "There is just
one positive feature of the Soviet system. That is its
historical mission. It serves as a negative example
to all peoples and nations. It is a grand experiment

which should serve to persuade everyone that the whole
theory of Marxism was wrong. That is its only redeeming
feature."

* * * * *

What about American foreign policy? The emigrés
were unanimous in their condemnation of technology trans-
fers to the Soviet Union, and almost equally critical,
with only a few reservations on humanitarian grounds,
of American wheat deals with Russia. "American foreign
policy must be as strong as possible. Deal from
strength. Don't believe in SALT. Soviets will deceive
the United States. Don't trust any documents signed
by the Soviet government. To them, it is just a piece
of paper, especially for the next Brezhnev."
    "America had the wrong policy right from the be-
ginning," an emigré engineer opined. "From the time
of intervention in the Civil War, it was a passive reaction; you didn't want to succeed. So the Revolution
survived. You gave the Soviets tremendous help under
NEP, and they nationalized your plants in return. Before
and during World War II, technology poured into Russia.
They never paid your banks; they owe eleven million dollars each year. And you keep pouring in your technology.
This is an easy policy--and the Soviet Union plays on
it as it grows in power. You should have stopped it
at the Revolution. But there was no ideology strong
enough to say a resounding 'NO' to the communists."

* * * * *

When asked to respond to a series of political
statements, the emigrés rejected without hesitation an
egalitarian pronouncement: "A good society is one which
strives to make men materially equal." No, people are
not equal, was the universal response. But what could
be made of the following statement? "People cannot be
free unless they are allowed to own property." When
rephrased several different ways, and illustrated with examples, I occasionally succeeded in making the meaning
clear to the emigré. It was a struggle, for as several
of the Russians admitted, they had never perceived a
connection between freedom and property. A few replied
that they would have to ponder this relationship, rather
than offering a facile response. One engineer struggled
somewhat dialectically with the thought: "Sure, people

can be free without property. Property makes people
not free because you're tied to it. People who don't
have property are more free than capitalists . . . .
But, on second thought, free enterprise is good, it must
be permitted; private property is necessary."

* * * * *

    Despite frequent warnings both from Americans pro-
cessing the Russian Jews and from the emigrés themselves
that the newcomers would be less than candid in answering our questions or even purposefully deceptive, we
found the opposite to be true. Most of our interviews
extended beyond the agreed-upon hour to sometimes three
or four hours of animated discussion. Rather than being
constrained or duplicitous, they seemed eager to display
their newly discovered freedom to criticize Soviet life
and American social mores. It was as though they had
been waiting for months or years since their arrival
in the United States for someone to come out and ask:
"What was it like to grow up, live, think, and work in
Soviet Russia?" Russians do love to talk about politics,
life, art, culture, and music on into the night in a
zestful, provocative way that escapes Americans of similar occupational and educational backgrounds. What they
regret most is the loss of the conviviality of trusted
friendships in Russia: "What surprised me most about
American life was the appearance. I didn't think it
would be so different from Russia and even Europe. No
people are on the streets. People sit at home in their
one-floor houses. In Russia we are closer, more friendly. We meet each other, like a family. We go out to
show off and admire our city, Leningrad. We go out on
the streets to be with people and to see people."
    To the interviewer, these displaced Russians seemed
gregarious, extroverted, and in a few cases, a trifle
garrulous, but never dull. Neither a beaten nor broken
people, these courageous individuals eagerly embrace their
new possibilities, to be truly alive for the first time,
and to be free. For some, growing up and living in
Russia casts an indelible shadow, one that they will
never lose, but for their children, life will be different, and infinitely better. This America of hope
for the next generation was the beacon that drew millions
of immigrants to our country, but it holds an added poign-
ancy when cherished by these outcasts from the Soviet

Gulag. The following sentiment was expressed by many emigres: "In Russia the entiré country is a prison. One cannot be truly alive as a human person in such a place."

Contributors

ALEXANDER DRANOV is a student at the Law School of the University of Pennsylvania. He graduated from the Moscow Institute of Foreign Languages and taught English at the Moscow Institute of Mining until he applied to leave the USSR.

JOSEPH DREW is Associate Professor in the Department of Political Science at the University of the District of Columbia. His background is in journalism and sociology and he earned his Ph.D. in the latter at the New School for Social Research. Prior to entering academia he worked as a congressional assistant. His particular research interest, in addition to Soviet Jewry, is social stratification.

STEPHEN C. FEINSTEIN is Associate Professor of History and Chair of the Soviet Seminar at the University of Wisconsin-River Falls. His Ph.D. is from New York University and he writes in the areas of Russian and Middle Eastern History, and Russian and Soviet avant-garde art.

JEROME M. GILISON is Dean of Undergraduate Studies at Baltimore Hebrew College. His doctorate, in Political Science, is from Columbia. For a decade he taught at Johns Hopkins. He has published several books on Soviet politics and has edited The Soviet Jewish Emigré.

ZVI GITELMAN is Professor of Political Science at the University of Michigan. He holds the Ph.D. from Columbia University. He is one of the pioneers in the study of the new Soviet migration, having carried out research both in the United States and Israel, and has written widely on that subject and others concerning the Soviet Union and Eastern Europe.

DAN N. JACOBS is Professor of Political Science at Miami University. His Ph.D. is from Columbia University.

175

He has published more than thirty books and articles, mostly in the areas of Russian and Chinese studies.

ELLEN FRANKEL PAUL is Assistant Professor of Political Science at the University of Colorado at Boulder and is an Associate at the Hoover Institution on War, Peace, and Revolution at Palo Alto, California. Her Ph.D. is from Harvard University. Her area of emphasis is political philosophy, in which she has written extensively, her most recent book being Moral Revolution and Economic Sciences.